D0188891

IT'S NICE TO MEET ME TOO

THE LAUGHTER AND LESSONS LEARNED FROM RAISING RANDY, A YOUNG MAN WITH TUBEROUS SCLEROSIS

IT'S NICE TO MEET ME TOO

THE LAUGHTER AND LESSONS LEARNED FROM RAISING
RANDY, A YOUNG MAN WITH TUBEROUS SCLEROSIS

Randy

CYNTHIA RUST

Cindy

— BEAVER'S POND PRESS —
MINNEAPOLIS, MN

It's Nice to Meet Me Too © copyright 2017 Cynthia Rust. All rights reserved. No part of this book may be reproduced in any form whatsoever, by photography or xerography or by any other means, by broadcast or transmission, by translation into any kind of language, nor by recording electronically or otherwise, without permission in writing from the author, except by a reviewer, who may quote brief passages in critical articles or reviews.

Edited by Robert Schmidt

ISBN: 978-1-59298-768-9
Library of Congress Catalog Number: 2017950324

Printed in the United States of America

First Printing: 2017
21 20 19 18 17   5 4 3 2 1

Book design by Athena Currier
Handwritten font by Phoebe Louks

Beaver's Pond Press, Inc.
7108 Ohms Lane
Edina, MN 55439–2129

(952) 829-8818
www.BeaversPondPress.com

For more information on this book, visit:
www.itsnicetomeetmetoo.com

TO RANDY . . . AND ALL
THE RANDYS OF THE WORLD

CONTENTS

PART II: THE "RANDY STORIES"

FOREWORD

NOW THAT WE'VE BOTH BECOME mothers ourselves, we give our mom a hard time for always responding to our parenting problems with, "I know, I know, I went through that too . . . *and I had Randy!*" It's not always the sympathy we're looking for when one of our kids has just tossed the car keys in the toilet or is acting very "seven-going-on-seventeen," but it is exactly the perspective we need. Because when we stop to think about it, it truly is an astounding realization. She did all this *and she had Randy*.

When our mom first asked us to write a foreword for her long-planned "Randy book," we knew we would have no shortage of things to say about the person who has been the most influential in our lives—our brother, Randy. The one who, from our very first days, has shaped our personalities in ways no one else could. But what this book will not tell you, at least not explicitly, is what an inspiration our mother always has been and continues to be. So we are setting aside the many, many thoughts we have about Randy (perhaps for a sequel?), and instead we are paying tribute to the pillar of our family—our mom, Cynthia.

To say that parenting Randy required patience, creativity, and an infinite amount of unconditional love would be an understatement. With the unwavering support of our dad, she has spent every day of Randy's thirty-eight-year existence advocating for better living accommodations, more extensive staff training and understanding, superior education and work opportunities, and more advanced drug therapies and medications to enhance his quality of life. She's been on a constant mission to better his never-ending childhood, all while maintaining her full-time job teaching special education for thirty-plus years, her forty-plus year marriage, her numerous close friendships, and even a few hobbies thrown in for good measure.

Above all, there is the fact that, in addition to the challenging task of caring for Randy, she and my dad also managed to raise us girls with a normal (as far as we knew) childhood. There was never a moment when either of us felt like we were receiving anything less than her full devotion and attention because of Randy's unique needs. She has always gone above and beyond for all three of us, every single day. This book is just one more example of a checked box on her "things to do for my children" list—a dedicated mother's love letter to her son. Randy will not have children or leave any significant contributions to science or business or art—his legacy will be the laughter and the lessons that are shared here, on these pages, through the eyes of his incredible mother.

Stephanie Rust Johnson & Allie Rust Rangel

PREFACE

THIS BOOK CHRONICLES THE life of Randy, a mentally handicapped young man, through stories that may make you laugh until you cry, while filling your heart with joy instead of sadness. Our family has always turned to humor as our coping mechanism and we have found that laughter is definitely the best reaction to Randy's most heartbreaking challenges, his frequently embarrassing outbursts, and his most outrageous behaviors. And—don't be fooled—Randy is fully in on the jokes. There is no doubt that the majority of what he does is completely intentional—and done with the goal to get a laugh. We tell our stories because we simply cannot stop laughing—not at him, but right along with him.

As we dive into the "Randy stories" later in the book, we hope you will enjoy them as much as we have. These stories have been told over and over, often taking on lives of their own. From family holidays, to my classrooms, to my daughters' groups of friends, these stories have circled the globe, occasionally even coming back to us. One time, my husband, Terry, was on the golf course and overheard someone he did not know telling one of our classic Randy stories. Another time, an acquaintance of my daughter Stephanie shared that she had been listening to a coworker tell a funny story when she had to interrupt to ask, "Is this a 'Randy Rust story'? A friend told me this same one years ago!"

By sharing our stories, my family and I hope to help others better understand our lives with Randy. The humor in these stories has served as a tool for breaking down people's uncertain and often uncomfortable attitudes towards the "Randys" of the world—and we hope it has also helped promote acceptance and appreciation for people of all different abilities.

These stories have also brought people closer to us and our situation. As a prime example of this, I have included the following email from one of the board members I worked with while organizing the annual Tuberous Sclerosis Walk in 2006.

> **From:** Sherri
> **To:** Cindy
> **Sent:** Thursday, May 04, 2006 12:25 PM
> **Subject:** Re:
>
> Cindy, best of luck in Cincinnati. I hope they are able to help Randy!! I think

everything is going pretty well for the walk. So far the weather looks like it will behave. We have a lot of walkers and teams signed up.

Let me know how everything goes. I'll talk with you soon.

Sherri

P.S. A funny story… A few years ago, my neighbor Karen told me stories about being a para at Champlin Park and how she walked into class one day and everyone was apologizing because one of the students had thrown her bike. We laughed about it. Well, recently, she was telling me how good the special ed teacher was at Champlin Park and I was saying you told me how good she was too. Then I said, "Oh, did you ever know Randy Rust?" She's like, "Oh my gosh, he's the one who threw my bike. He was a tough cookie." We were laughing. Small world, huh!!! She didn't ever work with him but knew of him…

Parents of handicapped children fight harder for them because we know that they are unable to fight fully for themselves. My family and I have been fighting for Randy for every single one of his thirty-eight years, and will continue to fight for him until the day we die. Everything we have done, we would gladly do again—but without laughter this fight would have been nearly impossible.

The stories in this book are our tribute to Randy—one small way of thanking him for bringing a nonstop sense of humor to our lives.

PART I

THE STORY
OF RANDY

THE JOURNEY BEGINS

HE DUE DATE FOR OUR child was November 7, 1978, but that day came and went along with many, many more. Randolph Jay Rust finally entered the world on November 29, 1978, and—from that moment on—Randy made it clear that he would never be predictable.

Up until Randy's birth, Terry and I thought we had everything in our lives figured out and planned perfectly. We had just bought our first home in Saint Paul, Minnesota, and were starting our careers—Terry as a certified public accountant and me as a high school special education teacher. Life was good and we were full of excitement about the arrival of our first child. Things were all going according to plan.

Weighing in at almost ten pounds and looking like the resident linebacker of the nursery, Randy was large and in charge from the very beginning. His bassinet was the only one with three makeshift pacifiers lining it, a clear sign that our son cried a lot. We would soon come to discover that it would take much more dramatic measures than a few baby bottle nipples stuffed with cotton to calm Randy.

Just as all new parents do, we examined every inch of our little bundle of joy. It did not take long for us to notice that Randy's left side appeared to be larger than his right and that his left eye was almost swollen shut. He also had a large white, ash-leaf "depigmented" area on his left leg—an abnormality unlike anything the staff at the hospital had ever seen.

My first concerned call was to my parents, who—aside from the obvious family connection—were both doctors in Iowa. We repeatedly asked my father, an ophthalmologist, what he thought could be wrong with Randy's eyelid. All he could do was suggest we talk to our doctors, and tell us that he would do some research on his own.

Questions, questions, and more questions piled up about our new baby—most of which went unanswered as our little family of three left the hospital and began the journey of a lifetime.

THE SEARCH FOR ANSWERS

THE FIRST FEW MONTHS OF Randy's life were spent driving back and forth, visiting specialists in different medical fields.

Particularly concerned about his enlarged left arm, the pediatrician suggested that Randy be examined by the University of Minnesota's oncology department. Upon glancing around the lobby, we noticed Randy was by far the healthiest looking baby there. It was a realization that gave us hope and, in hindsight, a lot of perspective. We were relieved to learn that he did not have cancer, but frustrated to be left with only a partial diagnosis of something with a name we had never heard before: lymphangioma. Our relief was tempered by our lingering questions.

Soon after our oncology appointment, my two months of maternity leave ended and I returned to teaching, feeling confident in the wonderful daycare we had ever-so-carefully selected for Randy. That daycare was short-lived, however, as they were simply unable to console Randy and calm his constant agitation. The next two daycares also failed to handle the excessive crying and, after three strikes, we were out of luck and without a plan. With our options narrowing—and the realization that group daycare was out of the picture—we looked for a full-time babysitter (what is now referred to as a nanny). We did not know it then, but that arrangement would also prove to be short-lived, as Randy's diagnosis was just around the corner.

Shortly after Randy's six-month diphtheria-pertussis-tetanus (DPT) shot, he began to have seizures, which resulted in numerous hospital visits, many new doctors, and even more new medicine trials. Treating Randy and managing his health quickly became a full-time job— my new full-time job—as I took a leave of absence from teaching.

As fall approached, so did Randy's nine-month benchmark appointment. Because of the seizures and the resulting hospitalizations, he was severely behind in terms of his overall development. To stop the prolonged and violent status seizures he was having, we had to administer what felt like an entire pharmacy of drugs and connect him to a respirator to help him breathe. During this time, Randy was hospitalized at the University of Minnesota Hospital where, finally, our questions were answered.

In September of 1979, Randy was diagnosed with tuberous sclerosis. As the Tuberous Sclerosis Alliance website defines it, tuberous sclerosis complex (TSC) is "a genetic disorder that causes non-malignant tumors to form in many different organs, primarily in the brain, eyes, heart, kidney, skin, and lungs. The aspects of TSC that most strongly impact quality of life are generally associated with the brain; seizures, developmental delay, intellectual disability, and autism. However, many people with TSC are living independent, healthy lives and enjoying challenging professions such as doctors, lawyers, educators, and researchers. The incidence and severity of the various aspects of TSC can vary widely between individuals—even between identical twins."[1]

At the time of his diagnosis, Randy had detectable tumors in his heart and brain and would eventually develop additional tumors throughout his lungs and—most aggressively—in his kidneys.

Some statistics we know now about TSC, which we did not know on that day in 1979:

- At least two children born each day will have tuberous sclerosis complex.

- Current estimates place tuberous sclerosis complex-affected births at one in 6,000.

- Nearly one million people worldwide are estimated to have TSC, with approximately 50,000 in the United States.[2]

---

1 "About TSC," *Tuberous Sclerosis Alliance*, http://www.tsalliance.org/about-tsc/what-is-tsc/, accessed February 21, 2017.
2 *Ibid.*

As a special education teacher, my past experiences included working in an autism unit at a hospital and teaching teenagers with emotional and behavioral disorders. I was very familiar with certain diseases and conditions causing mental retardation and autism, so although it is a rare disease, I had actually heard of tuberous sclerosis before and knew the extent of the damage that the seizures could cause. Even so, it was extremely difficult to absorb all the ramifications of the disease and how it could—and would—affect our family.

Randy's diagnosis day was the worst day of my life. Since I was young, I had always had a feeling that I would have a child with special needs and, on that day, my premonition became a reality. I can still vividly picture the weather that day—puffy white clouds floated in a beautiful autumn sky as my world filled with dark storm clouds.

The doctors immediately performed an array of tests on both Terry and me, from brain X-rays to skin and eye exams, to see if either of us had tuberous sclerosis. It was truly a blessing that neither of us had any signs of the disease—that way there was no silent blame or guilt placed on one parent over the other.

As we talked to the doctors, we realized that the prognosis was, in the best of terms, grim. We were told Randy would certainly be mentally handicapped and have autism, and would most likely have to be institutionalized. We were also informed that tuberous sclerosis is autosomal dominant, meaning that if one of us carried the gene, any future children we had would have a 50/50 chance of also having TSC. In the 1970s, however, there was no test for its genetic marker, so there was no way to definitively know if either of us was a carrier.

One thing in our favor was that the first book ever written about tuberous sclerosis had just been published in 1979, by Dr. Manny Gomez of the Mayo Clinic. After reading it cover to cover, multiple times, we took Randy to see Dr. Gomez in Rochester.

During those early years, Dr. Gomez and I became dear friends and served on the TSC board together. We would hold teleconferences, speak around the country, and I traveled to national neurology conventions, often working the tuberous sclerosis booth. I was dedicated to learning all I could about the disease, connecting with other parents of children with tuberous sclerosis, and helping to raise funds for further research. My highest hope was that someday someone would find the genetic marker.

STEPHANIE

THROUGH MY WORK ON THE board, I met other parents of children with tuberous sclerosis across the country. In getting to know them, I discovered that most had decided not to have any more biological children, and had either stopped having children or had chosen to adopt.

Terry and I were struggling, because we wanted to have more children, but Randy's diagnosis had been life altering. Dr. Gomez knew of our uncertainty and suggested we meet with Dr. Gorman, an oral surgeon at the University of Minnesota. He was known for his ability to diagnose a variety of genetic diseases from simply examining a person's mouth. So, we took Randy, who was one year old at the time, and went to have our mouths examined.

While we were certainly skeptical, we were hanging onto the slightest bit of hope for having more children of our own. With an optimistic attitude, his recommendation was to go ahead. At the same time, my mother was overseeing all of the medical school residents at the University of Iowa. One of her residents was pregnant and wanted to give her baby up for adoption. Though we had the opportunity to adopt this child, after meeting with Dr. Gorman we had made up our minds to try for a second biological child.

On August 21, 1981, Stephanie Marie Rust arrived. Little did this tiny newborn know about the family she had just been born into, or the big brother she would now protect forever.

While Stephanie's arrival was a blessing, her birth was hardly uneventful. In addition to a collapsed lung, the pediatric cardiologists thought she had dextrocardia, a condition where the heart is located on the wrong side of the body, which usually requires correction via a surgical procedure. We left the hospital with a warning to watch her closely for signs of heart issues, especially oxygen deprivation.

My mother, a family practice doctor, was not worried. From the beginning, she felt the heart specialists had read the X-ray wrong; she strongly believed that Stephanie's collapsed lung had pushed her heart over. After two months of monitoring both of our children for medical emergencies, we found out my mother had been right all along and were informed that Stephanie was perfectly healthy. After those few tense months passed, we were off to a great start with our new daughter, who was quickly nicknamed "Puff" by her older brother, who could not pronounce her real name.

As we watched the two of them grow, it seemed as though Stephanie was racing through her infancy to assume the role and responsibilities typically expected of an older sibling. In many ways, she actually benefited from participating in the various speech exercises that we were doing with Randy. While children with tuberous sclerosis can be nonverbal, I was determined that Randy would not be one of them.

Relying on my undergraduate degree in speech pathology from the University of Iowa, I recalled learning about an approach called "melodic intonation therapy," which is a method of teaching (or re-teaching) speech through rhythm and song. I believed that Randy could and would learn to speak, as he was already humming and singing. So our family began to sing everything we spoke and, within a year, both Randy and Stephanie were speaking in full sentences. I had been lucky enough to find a speech therapist familiar with this approach and we were both excited with the progress Randy made during that year.

Unfortunately, however, that year was also the official beginning of Randy's extensive vocabulary of swear words. Although we were not sure where he learned them (considering the relatively conservative language we used at home), we figured they caught his attention because of the heightened energy, drama, and volume that typically accompanied them. It also did not hurt that Randy was a natural-born comedian and learned quickly that swear words could usually earn him a bigger reaction, and more attention, from those around him. When Randy was four years old, during one hospital stay, a neurologist asked him how he felt. Randy responded, "Like shit." While we were a bit shocked by his choice of words, we had to admit that it was probably a pretty accurate answer, given the circumstances.

To this day, we are still not sure where he learned all of his swear words, but his sailor-like vocabulary has certainly reached far beyond what he ever heard at home. Obscenities aside, we were simply thrilled that his speech therapy was beginning to enable him to communicate his needs and wants to us, which was a huge accomplishment.

Little did we know that this was the key to unlocking the tsunami of Randy. We would soon learn, however, that once he started talking there would be no stopping him.

ALLISON

FROM A MEDICAL STANDPOINT, life was challenging for us over the next few years. Not only was Randy hospitalized frequently with status seizures, but also, in 1983, my mother suddenly became gravely ill and we had to pack up quickly and travel to Iowa to be with her when she passed. In a cruel twist of irony, Randy ended up having a status seizure about an hour after my mother died and ended up on the very same respirator she had just been on. As if the day could not get any worse for us, the small hospital in Iowa did not have a pediatric attachment for the respirator so my brother's friend, a pilot, flew to Rochester in the middle of the night to get one. Randy came very close to dying that night, and I strongly believed that my mother sent him back to me. (Well, either that or maybe heaven was just not quite ready for Randy yet.)

Soon after, Terry and I decided to ignore the risk factor yet again and have another child. On September 6, 1985, Allison "Allie" Marie Rust was born. She was perfectly healthy and truly completed our family. We were thrilled that Randy would have double the protection and care from his loving sisters.

Like most families, we became a tight-knit group, the five of us. Most of the time, family dinners proved to be a major struggle, but I chose to find the humor instead of the horror in mealtime. We always attempted to be a good Catholic family and say grace before meals. Around the time Randy was ten years old, Stephanie was eight, and Allison was four, Stephanie would start us off with the well-known blessing she said daily at her Catholic school; Allison would follow with a Jewish prayer she had learned from attending the Jewish Community Center preschool; and, lastly, Randy would stand and proudly recite . . . the Pledge of Allegiance.

As the baby of the family, Allison soon proved to be a bit feistier than Stephanie had been. She was not afraid to hit Randy back and let him know when she was unhappy with his behavior. At that point in time, Randy was very verbal, and incredibly repetitive, and he would respond to Allie's reactions by constantly singing, "I just don't like you Allisi-i-in." But, deep down, we could tell that his love for her was growing stronger each day.

Allison has always joked that "someday Randy will stand up from the dinner table, admit that this has all been an elaborate lifelong hoax, grab the car keys, and drive off into the sunset."

Both Stephanie and Allison are beyond compassionate with Randy and, as adults, they continue to look out for their big brother and include him in all of their own family gatherings.

THE SCHOOL OF RANDY

A s **RANDY GOT OLDER,** finding a good school for him became a new—yet familiar—challenge for our family to face. His first stop was our neighborhood public elementary school, where our attempts to include Randy in mainstream classes made history.

Mainstreaming him for music ended badly (and quickly) because, while Randy loved to sing loudly, he would only sing the songs he wanted to hear—which consisted exclusively of "The Star-Spangled Banner" and Christmas carols (no matter what time of year). Randy got lost or went missing many times in the building, only to be found in the kitchen trying to place a special lunch order of hamburgers and french fries. When served Sloppy Joes one day, he loudly announced to the cafeteria that his lunch looked "like diarrhea."

Randy had been receiving physical therapy and occupational therapy since he was two years old, but being in a regular public school was an adventure—for all of us. Even though we thought we knew what we were doing, just getting Randy to and from school on a daily basis was a challenge. The driver of his school bus learned quickly that Randy had no problem riding stark naked . . . but we'll talk more about that later.

Randy's Individualized Education Plan (IEP) meetings were extremely involved and often resembled a town hall assembly, as there was a huge team of people trying to figure out the best way to control his behaviors while still attempting to provide him with a solid education. It was always disturbing to count how many of the aides or teachers working with Randy came to these meetings bruised or bandaged due to his behavioral outbursts at school, yet it also helped us realize how much they truly cared about Randy's education.

Even with all of the ups and downs, Randy's memories of his elementary school are fond. To this day, we cannot drive past the school without Randy saying he wants to go back there. He asks about his teachers and remembers each and every one of them, frequently asking, "When can I be big again and go back?" (And yes, you read that correctly, he always confuses big with small.)

When Randy was in fifth grade, the school hired a new aide, Erich, to work directly with him. Erich was nothing short of a miracle worker with Randy, and for two years we were all amazed by his incredible growth and the improvement in his behavior. When Randy was twelve years old, after we had given the idea much thought and consideration, we decided to have Erich become Randy's foster parent. This decision meant that Randy would be placed with Erich at his home, with his young wife and new baby daughter. They lived less than a mile from our family, so we could easily bring Randy home on the weekends and for special occasions. Randy continued to respond to Erich in ways we had not even imagined were possible. Under Erich's care, Randy helped remodel their basement, took care of landscaping duties, and was even trusted to take their young daughter on stroller rides up and down their street, independently.

Unfortunately, this incredible arrangement did not last nearly as long as we hoped it would. Four years after Randy was placed in Erich's care, Erich died suddenly of an undetected heart ailment at the age of twenty-nine. The loss was devastating. Mainly, we grieved for the loss to his wife, his daughters—he had three by that time—and the rest of his family and friends.

But we also grieved for what could have been for Erich, as well as the life Randy could have led under Erich's care. Erich had recently submitted plans for a hobby farm, which was to become a group home for Randy and two other young boys in Dakota County. Erich and his family were going to devote their lives to the group home full time and they had hoped to provide an amazing life filled with opportunities for Randy and others like him.

We were all truly heartbroken as we restarted our search for Randy's next opportunity.

EENIE, MEENIE, MINEY GROUP HOME

AFTER RANDY'S PLACEMENT with Erich ended, we tried several different arrangements in group homes over the next five years. Each one proved to be an unsuccessful fit. These placements were filled with staff who were, quite frankly, completely unprepared for Randy's challenging behavior.

One unsuspecting group home manager learned this the very hard way, one day while driving down a busy street with Randy in the back seat. Randy, who had become unhappy with the ride for some arbitrary reason, grabbed the man's long ponytail and used it to start pulling him into the back seat of the car. Fortunately, there was a median in the road that the man was able to quickly pull his car onto before he was physically tossed out of the car onto it. Randy chased him on foot down that median until some well-meaning joggers called the Saint Paul police, understandably thinking Randy was attempting a carjacking. (I should mention that having the police called to a situation involving Randy was not a new experience, but the specific circumstances were certainly a first.)

When drivers' ponytails were not available, Randy frequently resorted to trying to get attention by punching out windows in the group home vans. This would most often lead to Randy being put into physical restraints by a staff member—as well as an accompanying (yet incorrect) "Vulnerable Adult Report" being filed to the State of Minnesota, typically by a Good Samaritan who assumed Randy had been the victim instead of the attacker.

Over the years, the group home staffs have spanned the full spectrum of humanity—in gender, race, religion, and background. It's safe to say that women have had it the roughest of each staff (and, therefore, have been few and far between). But by far some of the most memorable staff Randy ever had was during his time in a state-run group home called Rosewood in Dayton, Minnesota.

He was in Rosewood during the Minnesota state strike under Governor Jesse Ventura when the Minnesota National Guard was called in to cover shifts at the group home. It may not have been the perfect situation for many residents, but Randy has never had so much discipline in his life; every response included "Yes, ma'am" and "No, sir." (It made me think that, in another life, Randy would have made a wonderful military man.) But the honeymoon did not last forever and soon, being a state-run group home, Rosewood was being overloaded with clients from the state hospitals. So, once again, it was time to search for a new place for Randy.

Throughout our search, we interviewed numerous companies and visited several group homes. Eventually we found a home in a lovely new housing development, less than a half hour away from us, in a neighborhood full of nice, young families. We were so optimistic and, looking back, a little naive. We decided to host an open house to introduce the neighborhood to Randy and his new roommate, Johnny, hoping that the neighbors would feel more comfortable welcoming the boys in. Only one neighbor showed up. Even so, at first glance, I was excited to have someone actually come. The new neighbor seemed incredibly interested as she asked a ton of questions, and I was encouraged by what I thought was a sincere attempt to learn more about the boys and their diseases. Unfortunately, it turned out that she was gathering information not for herself, but for a petition that the neighborhood eventually submitted to have the group home removed from the area. Of course, by the time they filed the petition, we had to admit that we could see their side of the argument. After all, it was difficult to argue when Johnny streaked naked through a big neighborhood garage sale, causing a little bit of a scene.

As we moved on from that, options were beginning to feel limited and Randy was placed in a home with two other behaviorally challenged young men. We learned that, together, they ranked as the county's "top three most behaviorally challenged" clients. (Sadly, there were no trophies given out with that honor.) Unfortunately, but unsurprisingly, it did not lead to a healthy living environment for Randy. It did produce a few memorable stories, though.

While living at this home, we noticed that Randy's clothes seemed to be disappearing. One day I arrived to pick up Randy for a home visit and was greeted at the door by one of Randy's roommates . . . wearing all of Randy's clothes. When I commented, "Hmm, those look just like Randy's," he wordlessly responded by immediately removing all of them—and standing there in front of me, totally naked. I considered that to be his confession.

A classic tale of miscommunication also occurred while Randy was living in that home. At bedtime, Randy would not stay in his room. We were told that he repeatedly came out to complain to the night staff that there was a butterfly in his room. The staff ignored his complaints, telling him that a little butterfly could not hurt him. After a few more trips out of his room, and as Randy grew more and more adamant that this butterfly was really bugging him, the staff finally went to check it out. It turned out that a full-size bat had somehow gotten into Randy's room and was shrieking and flying around it. Now, had Randy still had the water bed that we had experimented with (it was supposed to help with his recurring sleep problems), he may have been able to put up a fight against that bat. After all, Randy eventually realized that he could puncture it and use it to spray water at his staff—which might have taken care of the bat, as well. (As you can imagine, however, not long after he learned that trick, he was back to a regular mattress.)

A few more serious incidents later, it was once again time to find Randy a new living situation. We really wanted Randy's next place to be closer to our home, and to have a maximum of three clients, if possible. We hoped that the chances for medicine errors and missing personal items—and clothing—would be greatly reduced in a more intimate setting. We interviewed and visited several group homes close to us, and really liked the Cantata house in Rosemount, which is about twenty minutes from our home. There was only one other young man in the home and it seemed like an ideal situation. One catch—the house manager was a woman.

The week before Randy moved into Cantata, the other client's parents moved him home. It was hard not to take that personally but, then again, Randy had quite a history; it was hard to blame them. A little nervous about Randy's past, we met with the staff and suggested that a male staff member be present at all times with the female manager, but they underestimated the seriousness of our request and insisted they were comfortable with the arrangement. It did not take long for Randy to promote himself to the position of dictator of Cantata. In his first week there, he managed to destroy almost everything breakable, including lamps and windows. During a particularly destructive spree one night, the glass from a broken window sliced his arm open, narrowly missing an artery, and an ambulance had to be called. When I was notified of the situation, I asked what staff member was with Randy in the ambulance, only to be informed that no one was with him. They explained to me that he had injured the female staff member badly enough that she was currently en route to a separate hospital.

The good news? From that point on, they took our suggestions much more seriously. And, even after that incident, Cantata decided to keep Randy and he is still there today, almost ten years later.

A few weeks after the trip in the ambulance, we celebrated Randy's twenty-ninth birthday with a party at the group home—cardboard over the windows and all. It was a surprise birthday party, but, then again, pretty much everything for Randy is a surprise. We invited family, friends, and past staff for the celebration and served food from McDonald's (Randy's favorite) for dinner—along with a cake with golden arches. As people arrived at Cantata, a few commented on how dark it was inside with the windows boarded up and no lamps. We were a little embarrassed and briefly tried to explain what had happened. Luckily, since we were surrounded by Randy's true friends, someone commented that "lamps are way overrated anyway" and no one mentioned it again.

The crime scene-like appearance of the house was soon overshadowed by Randy's best line of the night. When three lovely young ladies arrived and introduced themselves as past staff, Randy was so excited to see them that he exclaimed, "Some days you just get lucky!" A quote that perfectly describes the life of our Rand.

And we have gotten so lucky with Cantata. Toby is the reigning champion for the longest-lasting manager that Randy has ever had, and we feel so fortunate to have someone who has Randy's best interests at heart at the helm of his great care team. We know that Randy is incredibly skilled at pushing buttons and testing boundaries, so his near decade run at Cantata speaks volumes about Toby and the entire staff's dedication to working with us to provide Randy with comfort, security, and happiness.

— PART II —

THE "RANDY STORIES"

"RANDYISMS"

LIKE ANYONE ELSE, RANDY IS a complex individual. Over the years, we have struggled to find the best way to really describe Randy to those who do not know him. He is hardly someone who can be summed up in a typical "elevator speech" (hence, the need for an entire book to fully portray the wild world of Randy). What makes him so unique are all of his distinctive quirks, his unusual sayings, his peculiar obsessions, and his somewhat bizarre habits—in short, his "Randyisms." Here are just a few of our favorites, to help provide a glimpse into life with Randy.

Randy has spent his life renaming people, or calling people "the other Mary," or "the new Mary" (who is always preferred to "the old Mary"). How he hears (or mishears) someone's name the very first time is how he will remember it forever. His cousins, who are triplets (and are now in their mid-twenties), still endure being called, "Baby Maggie," "Baby Anna," and "Baby Harry."

Here is a list of some of our favorite Randy name and phrase "translations":

RANDYISM | ## REAL WORLD TRANSLATION

RANDYISM	REAL WORLD TRANSLATION
Bob Dylan	Dylan
Boston	Steve (Boston is his hometown)
Breada	Greta
Brick	Rick
Calcium	Kelsey
"Clinton is a peach"	"Clinton is impeached"
Cocky puck	Hockey puck
Danny	Annie
Ebelyn	Evelyn
Kitty Cat	Kat
Mary and Wayne's husband	Mary and Wayne
Nancycaitlin	Nancy and Caitlin (He uses the same term for both people)
Puff	Stephanie
Roberta	Robert
Ronster	Ron
Rose Ann	Mary Ann
Rotten potatoes	Au gratin potatoes
"Scare me to desk"	"Scare me to death"
Shelagh	Sheila
Show and Tells	Hotels
Snow White and the Seven Doors	Snow White and the Seven Dwarfs

Spaghetti	Betty
Strawberry	Katie
The other Mary	Most women named Mary
Torah and Fargo	Torry and Margaux
Two squirrels	Tuberous sclerosis
Whitney Spears	Brittany
You been bowling	Bolla

Randy remembers my late mother, his grandmother, as "Mamie." When I became a grandmother in 2009, it was decided that I would be called "Mamie" and Terry would be "Pops." So when our granddaughter, Samantha, was over at our house and asked, "Where's Mamie?" Randy looked right at her and replied, "Mamie's dead!" You can imagine Samantha's relief—and my confusion—when I later entered the room.

In November of 2016, as Randy celebrated his thirty-eighth birthday, we also had Allison's in-laws over to celebrate her grandfather-in-law Hank's ninety-third birthday. Now, when Randy was young, we had a beloved golden retriever who was also named Hank, with whom Randy shared every single one of his ice cream cones. When we finished singing "Happy Birthday" to both Randy and Hank, Randy exclaimed, "Hank is dead!" This was news to Hank, obviously, and became another prime example of the "only one person/animal per name" rule in Randy's world.

In recent years, a lot of male staff from Africa have been hired at Randy's group home. Not long ago, I picked

Randy up for a home visit and was greeted by a new staff member, so I asked Randy the gentleman's name. Randy looked puzzled and began to name all of the other staff, and even some previous staff. When the new staff member just shook his head, Randy threw up his hands in exasperation and said, "Well, it's not Oprah!"

The Cantata staff have occasionally been confused about what Randy actually calls himself as well. (And for good reason.) At one point, Randy spent months telling them he did not want to be "Randy Rust" any longer, and that he wanted to be "Tom the brick man." It took us all *quite* a while to figure out exactly who "Tom the brick man" was—or where that idea came from. Finally, one day, he was watching TV and Tom Brokaw came on the news. That is when Randy excitedly yelled, "There's Tom the brick man!"

Whether it is renaming himself or telling you what things are called, Randy can be very convincing when he wants to be. For example, he spent years telling people that his sisters lived in a Boston group home when they were really attending Boston College.

Another example of this occurred on a family trip to Hawaii in 2009, when Randy's newest obsession had just become "bat whales" (aka *whales*—good old regular whales). Where the term *bat whales* came from, well, your guess is as good as mine. Even so, while we were on a family whale-watching excursion, Randy could not stop talking about the bat whales. As the first whale emerged from the water, Randy jumped up and screamed, "There's a bat whale! Woo-hoo! Bat whalesssss!" Which he then repeated every time a whale was spotted. It was not long before people began to come up and ask us what this new bat whale species was all about.

A man of strong convictions, Randy has never held back when expressing his opinion, either. Sensitive to smells, Randy hardly sugarcoated his view of my brand-new perm when he was about ten. As soon as I entered the house, Randy came right up to me with a disgusted expression on his face and said, "Ugh. Fix it, Mom; it hurts my eyes and smells like rotten eggs."

It is Randy's lack of filter—and the comments that it produces—that gives us the silver lining of his grandmother's hearing impairment. She is very hard of hearing, so between that and Randy's often-inappropriate comments, some pretty entertaining conversations take place between the two of them. One of the exchanges that I was lucky enough to overhear was a grown Randy informing his grandmother "I like to play with myself," and his grandma letting him know how proud she was of him for doing that. (See? Silver lining.)

However, his *great*-grandmother had perfect hearing. When he was very young, he was chatting with her when he suddenly reached out and swung the loose skin under her arm declaring it to be "just like Dumbo!" Great-grandma heard—and understood—that clear as a bell.

Another example of a typical conversation with Randy was one we had about a table in his group home that had somehow been broken. When I asked him if he wrecked the table, his answer was an incriminating "Well, I tried not to."

For reasons we have never fully understood, Randy has always had an obsession with towels and blankets. As a little boy, he would sit for long periods of time "sculpting blankets"—piling and shaping them into different creations. (This was such a unique pastime that it inspired Randy's great-aunt Ruth to create a sculpture of Randy sculpting blankets.) As an adult, this habit has morphed into wrapping blankets and towels around his head and face, especially while on long car rides. We have hypothesized that it is a self-soothing tool he uses when he is overstimulated, but if you dare ask him what he is doing he is very quick to respond: "Nothing." But, hey, we all get a kick out of watching the expressions of people passing by in other cars when they catch a glimpse of him in the back seat.

A less-endearing towel story centers on a beautifully embroidered hand towel. When Randy was about ten, he accompanied me to pick up his sister Stephanie from a play date she had with a new little friend from school. As we drove up to their beautiful home, Randy began to whine about having to go to the bathroom, which with Randy is always an urgent situation. Even though I did not know the mom well (and she definitely did not know Randy), she graciously let Randy use their bathroom as the rest of us waited in the foyer of their lovely home. When Randy finally emerged, he handed me a dirty embroidered hand towel while announcing that he could not find any toilet paper. That marked our first—and final—play date with that family.

We are grateful that Randy has, for the most part, outgrown his other frustrating bathroom habits. As a child, anything not nailed down was at risk of being flushed down the toilet. We would hear his telltale "Bye-bye!" coming from the bathroom followed by the inevitable—and too soon for us to stop—*flush*.

He does still put plenty of things in places where they do not belong, though. Once, while riding home from the cabin, he asked for a garbage bag. When no one responded right away, he looked around the car and said, "Oh, there you go." I turned just in time to see him throw the remains of his shake from Dairy Queen into my brand-new Louis Vuitton purse.

While ice cream is usually a pretty safe bet (even if he doesn't always finish it), he is less open-minded about other foods. If anyone comes to visit and is kind enough to bring food, he will inevitably ask, "Is this good or yucky?" And, don't worry, he will let everyone know what he has decided after tasting—or sometimes simply smelling—the dish.

One good example of his strange dietary habits: he detests butter. He will obsessively ask for the "raw butter" to be removed from the table. He cannot bear to look at it, much less taste it. He is okay with it if the butter is mixed into macaroni and cheese or brownie batter, but if he catches a glimpse of it going in, he will require multiple firm confirmations that the butter has melted away before he will eat it.

His strange dietary habits, combined with his daily medicine "cocktail" and the binge eating that it can induce, causes frequent stomachaches and bathroom visits. Randy is far from shy about letting everyone know about his stomach issues. Once, in the middle of a haircut, he urgently and dramatically shouted to us from across the salon, "I am going to have diarrhea!" We may never know whether this specific incident was caused by him eating an entire bunch of bananas, a full box of donuts, or simply a dab of butter but regardless, it was a dramatic—and very public—result.

Not everything that Randy says is cringeworthy; some comments are just endearingly *unique*. When Randy is expecting someone and they happen to be running late, Randy will wait at the window and repeatedly ask, "Did they lose themselves?"

And others are just plain understatements, to say the least. One day while we were spending time with family out at my brother and sister-in-law's house, Randy was alone in the kitchen for a few minutes, obsessively going through the ad section of their Sunday newspaper—most likely searching for a good deal on an MRI machine or water tower. Obviously not finding what he was looking for, he flung a page down onto the kitchen counter, right on top of a small, lit candle. As the paper caught fire and started flaming, Randy nonchalantly walked out onto the deck and announced to his dad and uncle, "It's getting a little hot in the kitchen." Thankfully we have learned not to take Randy's statements at face value and, upon investigating, they quickly put out the growing fire.

And then there are his most famous "Randyisms," which he uses on a daily basis:

- "In another lifetime I can have _____."
  (Insert "a water tower," "my own MRI machine," "a sleepover with *Entertainment Tonight* star Mary Hart," etc. here.)
- "Why can't I live at home forever?"
- "Adults cannot live with their moms."
- "Can I kiss your beak?"

A little further explanation of that last one: despite his other autistic tendencies, Randy has always been very affectionate, frequently showing much warmth toward his loved ones. He loves to kiss people affectionately on a specific spot on the top of their heads—their "beaks." People often mistakenly (but understandably) think he is referring to the nose, but we welcome this small misunderstanding in comparison to what he originally named the spot. He used to refer to it as "your crack" (we think—and *hope*—this was in reference to the location where people part their hair) but his staff worked hard to change "your crack" to something . . . *anything* . . . else.

My friend Mary loves to tell her Randy story of when she was introducing us to her dentist before an appointment that she had kindly set up. Mid-conversation, Randy turned to me and unmistakably asked, "Mom, can I kiss your crack?" You can see why we think that "beak" is a great improvement—it is a little strange no doubt, but definitely less disturbing in public.

While the list of Randy's odd tendencies literally grows daily, every once in a while he catches us off guard with something so completely right on and, well, *normal.*

One night when all of the grandchildren were over for a family dinner, I asked their parents "Can the kids each have a C-O-O-K-I-E?" Randy—who, as far as we know, has never come close to learning to read—promptly answered "I want a cookie!"

Another time, the whole family was spending the weekend at the cabin and headed over to a pancake breakfast at the local fire station. The kids were all exploring the fire trucks on display, climbing in and out, when Terry pointed to the driver's seat of the fire truck and asked Randy, "Want to jump in there?" Randy thoughtfully crossed his arms, shook his head, and responded, "Eh, I'm not a very good driver." *Right.* Let's all hope he never decides to change his answer on that.

TALKING TO STRANGERS

THERE IS SOMETHING REALLY entertaining about watching Randy interact with strangers. We have watched many unsuspecting people try to decipher and respond to Randy's bizarre comments and questions. When we are feeling generous, we jump in and apologize immediately—or at least try to explain the "Randyisms." But, when we are distracted (or perhaps just in need of a good laugh), we may give it a minute or two before interrupting. Here are a few of the gems that he has bestowed on random people:

- "Please take me to Target and buy me a new neck."
- "I don't like stinky underwear. Do you?"
- "When can I take J.Lo out for a beer?"
- "Hey, can you hook me up with a sandwich?"

- "Fix my itchy ears."
- "My butt is really itchy. Can you put some cream on it?"

As you can imagine, this is just a very short list of the unusual and not-always-appropriate questions and comments he directs at people he does not know. Occasionally, he takes it even further.

One year, when our family went to the Minnesota State Fair, Randy and I were sitting at a table by the big slide as everyone else was getting drinks and hot dogs. Soon a family of four sat down, using the other end of the table. The mother, father, and sister were somewhat overweight, but the boy next to Randy was extremely large. They had only been sitting for a minute or two when Randy reached over and began poking his finger in and out of the boy's belly. I was mortified . . . and frozen. Then, to really drive home his point, Randy asked, "Mom, can I be a *big* boy just like him?" I am sure that family did not share a table with anyone else for the rest of the day.

Though he does not read, Randy is truly a man of the twenty-first century, and even has a Facebook account. He logs on using an iPad we gave him so that he could listen to music and look at family pictures. The staff at the group home generally helps him with his electronics but, on a recent weekend visit, we took a look through it to update it and add some apps and pictures. Much to our surprise, when we checked on his Facebook profile we saw that he had received numerous friend requests from unfamiliar women who were very scantily clad in their profile pictures. Being more Facebook-illiterate than Randy, Terry and I had to enlist the help of our son-in-law to "unfriend" these gals.

Impressively, the naughty language began before he was even verbal.

Randy's most loyal childhood companion, Hank.

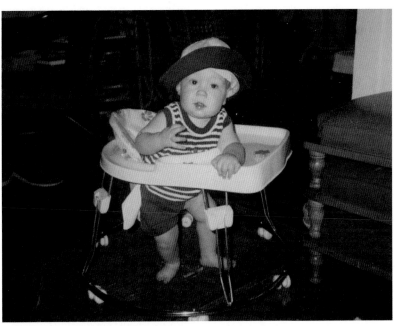

Anchors away with this nauti kid.

All aboard the Randy train. It's been a wild ride from the very beginning.

Beach babe.

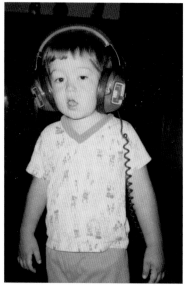

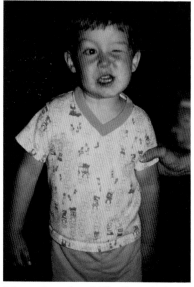

The start of his love for music and knack for misinterpreting lyrics.

Mastering the skill of a subtle wink. He still uses this party trick frequently.

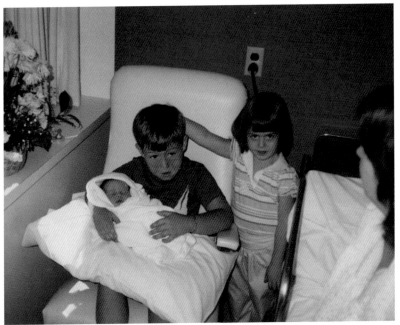

Meeting his baby sister, Allison, in September of 1985. Not exactly love at first sight but thirty-plus years later, he just adores her.

Shopping in the backyard for McDonald's hamburgers and french fries.

Pure admiration of Winnie's "big head."

The three musketeers, ready for takeoff.

We never did determine the inspiration for Randy's hobby of "molding" blankets and towels (and occasionally wearing his creations on his head).

"And a water tower, and new sheets, and a lot of black shirts, and a washing machine . . ."

Randy's preferred way of riding in cars—with a towel over his head and occasional breaks for orange pop and a quick browse through the "coupon ads."

One of Randy's favorite black shirts.

A man and his chick.

Halloween 2011. Randy as one-half of the award-winning costume duo, "Fork & Spoon." The crowd ate it up.

The group home staff took him shopping and let him choose his own costume. The winning selection? "Purple witch."

A stickler for
water safety.

Sometimes the caption just writes itself.

Who knew a giant, gray monorail pole would be the #1 attraction at Disney World? We did.

Randy and Mickey casually catching up on the obituaries.

"Shushing" Mom down the aisle at Stephanie and Erik's wedding.
December 2006.

Stephanie & Erik's wedding. December 2006.

Allie & Jesse's wedding. November 2012.

Cracking himself up with his nephew Brady. Christmas 2014.

Sharing his love of the cabin with his nephew Wes. Summer 2016.

The ever-elusive two thumbs up for his thirty-eighth birthday celebration.

Randy and his (temporary) bedfellow, Mr. Bubbly Thing.

Randy became a new obstacle on the mini golf course when he wouldn't leave the gorilla's side. September 2015.

Hoppy Easter 2017. With nieces Lynnie (left) and Samantha (right).

"Baby Breada." Randy and his niece Greta. Spring 2017.

Winning the title of "the fun uncle" came naturally.

Team Rand the Man marches on at the annual Step Forward to Cure TSC event. June 2017. Pictured from left to right: Lynnie Johnson, Stephanie Rust Johnson, Erik Johnson, Wes Johnson, Terry Rust, Randy Rust, Samantha Johnson, Cynthia Rust, Greta Rangel, Jesse Rangel, Brady Rangel, Allie Rust Rangel.

TALKING TO KIDS

WATCHING RANDY INTERACT WITH children can also be a very interesting, but thankfully *usually* less offensive, experience. He does not understand the concept of children being different ages, or the corresponding fact that, developmentally, babies are not equivalent to adults.

When Randy's nephew Brady was about six months old and innocuously swinging in his swing, Allie's husband, Jesse, kidded, "Hey, Randy, Brady's looking at you!" Randy looked over at little Brady, considered this for a minute, took a serious tone and asked, "You trying to start something with me, Brady?"

And once, in a misguided attempt to get help with a TV remote that was not working, he presented it to his two-year-old niece Samantha with the demand "Fix it." He just looked confused when she tried to explain, "I am only two, Randy." It still has not clicked for him. Since then he has even asked his niece Lynnie (a one-year-old at the time) to get down out of her high chair and go pour him some milk.

Despite their inabilities to meet all of his demands, Randy truly seems particularly energized and excited when surrounded by his little nieces and nephews. Whenever a new baby is expected and the ultrasound picture is passed around, we love hearing Randy's guesses as to what it is. Spicing it up beyond the typical guesses of "boy" or "girl," Randy has been known to offer up more creative answers like "a pizza" or "a raccoon." But he's no dummy; he is fully aware that more babies mean more birthday parties to celebrate—and more toys to play with.

Randy's nieces and nephews all love their uncle Randy—except for one trait. We are currently attempting to get Randy to stop calling his nieces and nephews "Baby _____" and just use their names. He especially struggles with his niece Evelyn's name, as she always gone by the nickname "Lynnie." When we tried to explain to Randy that he should call her Lynnie, he took one look at her and said, "She sure looks like Baby Ebelyn to me." Our attempts at changing this habit are proving to be an ongoing battle—and, most likely, one we will not win. While a big part of this is simply his rigid and stubborn nature, I believe that there is also a wistful underlying reluctance on his part to accept the fact that everyone around him is constantly growing up, while he stays frozen in his development.

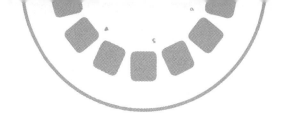

TALKING TO ANIMALS

RANDY HAS ALWAYS SPOKEN to animals as if they are humans. As I mentioned earlier, we had a golden retriever named Hank who was by Randy's side for the first ten years of his life. They were inseparable, the best of buds, and could often be seen sharing the same Popsicle or ice cream treat out in our backyard—one lick for Randy, one lick for Hank.

Hank was the sweetest dog and a neighborhood favorite—even inspiring the family next door to adopt a look-alike golden retriever. After the very sad day when Hank passed away—and once the neighbors' dog had grown to be full-size—Randy started a routine of "finding" their dog in their yard and escorting him back to our house, calling him Hank the whole way. We had to return him many times. I sincerely believe that Randy never quite grasped the truth that it was simply not Hank. To this day, if we pass a golden retriever, Randy excitedly points out, "There's Hank!"

Randy never developed the same bond with Hank's successors. His conversations with our Portuguese water dog, Hattie, mainly consisted of him telling her sternly, "If I've told you once, Hattie, I've told you a million times: do not pee in the yard. You need to pee in the bathroom." He obviously felt the same rules that applied to him should also apply to her.

It was not just dogs that Randy thought needed to learn these rules. Randy has never fully comprehended the nature and habits of any animals he meets. A former group home staff member owned a farm with horses that she enjoyed taking Randy out to visit. She told us that she could not contain her laughter when she overheard Randy yelling at a horse, "Do not poop there! Ick, use the bathroom!"

The horse, it seemed, did not understand him any better than Hattie had.

TALKING TO RANDY

RANDY OFTEN SPEAKS TO himself and about himself in the third person. We have read that is a sign of intelligence. Whether that is true or not, it does usually prove to be pretty effective in upping the comedic ante on his ridiculous statements.

Once, while seated next to me on an airplane, he rearranged himself, moving his legs to a more comfortable position. With sincere gratitude, he told himself, "Thank you for moving your legs; that was sure nice of you." (No one compliments Randy better than Randy!)

He has also been overheard promising himself many things, such as "When Oprah tells you it's okay to sleep in her bed, then Randy can sleep there." And when anyone utters the normal greeting that it is "so nice to see him," his standard response is "It IS nice to see me." And, as you may guess from the title, when first introduced to someone, Randy's typical response is the self-affirmation, "It's nice to meet me too."

Most often, however, Randy's third-person narrative comes out when he is being questioned on his behavior:

- "Who threw those lamps out the window? Randy threw the lamps."
- "Who broke all the heads off of the Barbie dolls? Randy did."
- "Where did all the cookies go? Randy ate them."
- "Who threw the TV down the stairs? Randy Rust did that."

Every once in a while he tries to assert a third person denial even *before* an accusation has been made. He has been known to exit the bathroom and proudly announce: "Randy did not overflow the toilet." Which, obviously, results in us all immediately jumping up and running to the bathroom.

FOUR-LETTER WORDS

OR A PERSON WHO—as we were warned by the doctors—would likely spend his entire life unable to communicate verbally, Randy is unbelievably expressive and vocal. His language is at different times sweet, entertaining, brutally honest—and peppered with expletives.

On a shopping trip to Target, Randy and I went down a toy aisle where a young mother was angrily reprimanding her young child. It was the kind of situation we have all encountered—where everyone witnessing the situation is uncomfortable and probably thinking "Someone should really say something." Well, Randy certainly is someone. We made our way past them and, just as I thought we were in the clear, Randy turned back around. He looked the woman straight in the eye and, in no uncertain terms, told her "Shut the fuck up."

Another example of his affection for that phrase involved Randy's high school principal. Randy was busy stacking pop cans in the vending machine, his assigned job, when the principal walked by and complimented him for a job well done. Completely annoyed by the interruption (even though it was praise), Randy disgustedly responded with "Shut the fuck up." The principal himself later told me the story, adding that Randy was the only student who could say that to him without getting suspended. (The principal's affection for him was particularly beneficial for Randy that week considering that it was the second time in just a few days that Randy had committed suspension-worthy behavior. A few days earlier, Randy had pulled the fire alarm at school—just to see what would happen—causing a full evacuation and the arrival of three fire trucks.)

As for anyone working with Randy, there was a steep learning curve for teachers and aides lucky enough to encounter Randy—and his language—in the school system. Whenever a new aide was hired, he or she would receive an extensive briefing about the seriousness of Randy's grand mal status seizures—but they may also have needed a language warning.

Once, one of the new aides—who was aware of the seizures, but less aware of Randy's typical bathroom behaviors—grew worried when Randy was in the bathroom stall for an extended time and would not answer him. Finally, after the aide resorted to attempting to open the stall door, Randy bellowed, "Leave the door shut, you asshole!"

No matter how extensive the preparations, working with Randy always requires a substantial amount of "on the job training" *and* a thick skin when it comes to swearing.

SMOOTH OPERATOR

WHEN **R**ANDY MOVED OUT OF our house and in with his school aide, Erich, we began the tricky task of teaching him to talk on the phone in order to stay close and ease the transition. Since Randy is a creature of habit with obsessive-compulsive disorder (OCD), we have had pretty much the same conversation with him every night over the past twenty-five years. That said, the calls have developed into more of a conversation and less of an interrogation over the years (our old "conversations" were almost entirely "What did you have for dinner? Were you good at school?").

Some of the most entertaining conversations we have with Randy center around his complaints about the staff at his group home. He will often report to me that he has fired one of them or ask, "Can they get fired?" But, at the same time, he is quick to rat himself out for bad behavior as well, telling us "I am not suppose to hit John" or "I was naughty today and lost my sausage." At other times his confessions have been less direct. One night while we were on the phone he was complaining of a sore throat, so I asked him if he felt sick. He replied, "No, I just shouldn't scream 'sons of bitches' over and over. It makes my throat hurt."

Typically, he only wants to talk to me during these calls. If I am gone or busy, he will repeatedly ask for me and, eventually, will just hang up on Terry or the girls. There is no question that he will always be a "momma's boy."

In general, Randy's nightly calls consist of letting me know what he did that day, the things he ate, and a full report on his health status. I have learned to interpret what he is telling me, filtering out the ailments to determine whether or not they are urgent. If he says he has "bumps on his head," it means he has a headache. "Coconuts in his throat" signal a sore throat. "Potatoes in his ears" tell us his allergies are acting up and he needs to have his ears cleaned out. Telling us that his "bones hurt" . . . well, we never have nailed down exactly what that one means.

It can be difficult for all of us when he is homesick and tells me that living at his group home is "too hard." He sometimes cries that the home "is giving me a headache" and begs me to come get him. He wants to come home and live with us forever—and he asks about it every night. But when I level with him that if he lived at home with me, full time, then *I* would have to go live at the group home for a break, he will relent, saying "Well, we don't want that!" Though most of his nightly calls are simply the same topics over and over, from time to time they can be heartbreaking. Still, every phone call ends with Randy telling me "I don't want to hang up on you, Mom," as he keeps me on the line as long as he can.

I have learned, over time, that I am not the only one Randy has a hard time saying goodbye to. We have been lucky to find some really wonderful, caring staff members over the years who Randy has grown very emotionally attached to. Many of these staff members have relayed stories of telling Randy goodbye at the end of their shift only to have him plead with them not to go home. When they try to reason with him and explain that they have to go take care of their children, Randy often responds with "Just throw your kids away so you can stay here."

We try our best to keep open lines of communication with the staff of any group home (or hospital, or anywhere else he might be going)—interpreting different "Randyisms" for them and making them aware of his likes and dislikes. Because he has such strong opinions regarding food, I used to try to be diligent about making those known to any new staff—until he started making a liar out of me. I would tell the staff to only order him hamburgers (because he detested cheese), but then he would tell the staff that he exclusively ate cheeseburgers.

It seems that whenever people get a little too comfortable with their knowledge of him or become overly confident in their ability to handle him, he takes it as a challenge to completely pull the rug out from underneath them. Once, when I was discussing Randy's violent out-bursts with some staff, they specifically asked if he was ever physically violent towards me. I was quick to answer "No, not with me" but—as soon as I had finished my sentence—Randy kicked me so hard in the shin that I fell to the ground. (As you might guess, we have learned to answer some of those questions in private . . .)

BEDROOMS

SINCE RANDY HAS SO FEW material things that he truly cares about, we have always tried our best to make his bedroom a place that is special and custom designed for him.

When he was about twelve, Randy talked obsessively about wanting mountains in his bedroom. He wanted real mountains right there in his room—and the bigger the better. Our solution was to find someone willing to paint an entire mountain scene on his wall, which is still there today. The joy he has gotten from his "mountain room" has been priceless.

Years later, when I was still teaching high school, a light bulb went off when a very talented and artistic student of mine was brainstorming different ways to earn extra money over the summer. We hired her to paint a scene from Randy's all-time favorite book, *Goodnight Moon*, on one wall of his bedroom at the group home, which he has now dubbed his "*Goodnight Moon* room."

DOCTORS, HOSPITALS, AND EMERGENCY ROOMS, OH MY!

To say Randy has spent a lot of time in doctors' offices and hospitals would be a vast understatement. Beginning with the concerns we had to address just after he was born and tracking to the present day, the total is currently at seventy-five hospitalizations and over thirty surgeries.

To this day, as Randy waits in the lobbies for his doctors' appointments he likes to "earn" (as he refers to it) a magazine for good behavior. As soon as we check in, he asks the receptionist at the front desk just how many magazines he can earn. Unless it is a repeat appointment and they recognize him, they are never quite sure how to answer and look to us for clues. We have all become uniform in our answer of *one* magazine per visit. Despite his repeated asking, we stick to that number. If we ever diverged from that answer, Randy's collections of "lobby magazines" would put him in serious contention for being featured on the reality show *Hoarders*.

We are always hopeful for as little time in the lobby as possible, because Randy's conduct creates lots of head turns and eye rolls—and can be a bit exhausting. When there are televisions, Randy always wants to change the channel (he is a chronic channel surfer and—when given the chance—never leaves a television on the same channel for longer than five seconds).

If the lobby has a particularly nice TV, we move into the more dangerous territory of Randy wanting to take the TV home with him. He will stand as close as possible to any wall-mounted TV, touch it, and examine the back of it (as if to see how easy it would be to remove). In essence, Randy has never outgrown the toddler's first rule of ownership: "If I want it, it's mine." (If there are no TVs, he will settle for being in control of the light switches, which can also be a "fun" challenge in public areas.)

As you might have guessed from some of the previous stories, Randy has always had a particular fascination with larger people—and a weakness for pretty blondes. As such, we always sit in the waiting rooms in silent anguish waiting for him to yell out "Can I be big like that man?" or "Can I take that pretty girl home with me?" Trying to keep him looking at magazines, while simultaneously keeping him from taking other people's magazines, is always the key for distracting him.

A particularly memorable waiting room story happened at one of Randy's allergy appointments. Randy and I were waiting with one of Randy's group home staff members, a wonderful young man named Ronald (who happens to be African American) who thankfully has an equally wonderful sense of humor. The three of us were sitting in a particularly crowded room as Randy paged through a magazine, stopping on a page with rainbow-colored children all wearing multicolored clothing. Without warning, Randy asked us loudly, "Can I be a colored boy, too?" Ronald and I could not contain our laughter, despite the disgusted looks coming our way.

It probably comes as no surprise that Randy has also had several visits to emergency rooms on holidays. One noteworthy visit happened on a particularly eventful Thanksgiving, when a piece of turkey needed to be surgically extracted from his nose. (I'll save you the details on that one.)

Randy's favorite hospital—because when you have had over seventy-five hospitalizations, you begin to play favorites—is Children's Hospital in Saint Paul. Having aged out of Children's, his preferred hotel—I mean, *hospital*—is now United. Upon check-in, he typically asks for a room with a view of "his cathedral" because, again, when you are a frequent customer, you come to expect some perks, and Randy loves that view.

His early hospitalizations were the most intense and were usually in the intensive care unit, with a private room. We try to be proactive and ask for a single room whenever he is admitted, but we are usually told there are none available. Lately, because of this, he has been placed in double rooms.

As you might guess, he also obsesses over the remote control for the shared TV in the room, changing the volume and channels incessantly. Suffice it to say, Randy is a less-than-ideal roommate. Because of his vast hospital experience, he knows how uncomfortable IVs and other (*ahem*) "tubing" can be, so he often tries to make the other patient in the room feel better—by removing those pesky apparatuses for him.

We always find it entertaining how single rooms rapidly (almost magically) become available right after Randy tries to play doctor.

During one of Randy's longer stays in an epilepsy unit, he developed a close bond with a lovely nurse named Grace. Grace was gentle, kind, and very patient. But even sweet Grace had her limits. Randy pushed her right past them the day he chose visiting hours to walk down the hallway—naked as the day he was born—singing out: "Gra-a-ace, I'm ready for my bath!"

As I have previously mentioned, one of Randy's obsessions is with overweight men with large stomachs. Not only does he notice them, but he actually often tells everyone that he wants to rub their stomachs. When he was about twenty-four years old, Randy was hospitalized at St. Mary's Hospital in Rochester for a ventricular tachycardia (V-tach) assessment.

One evening, the nurses offered to help Randy with his shower so Terry and I could take the girls downstairs for a quick dinner break. When we returned, we found the nurses running frantically from room to room—looking for Randy. Because the situation needed very little explanation, we joined the search. Much to our horror, we found Randy in a room at the end of the hall, sitting at the bedside of a very large man—rubbing his belly. (At least he was dressed!) It's a small miracle that no lawsuits resulted from that incident.

Randy's surgeries were always unique experiences, as well. When he was about thirteen and having a major surgery, he insisted on having his American Girl doll "Samantha" with him. (He had to have his own Samantha doll because Stephanie had one.) So Samantha accompanied teenaged Randy to surgery—and came out all stitched up and bandaged as well.

Randy has also made some very strange requests to the doctors before heading into the OR. Most often, he would ask them to give him a new neck, a new head, new toes, and to "make him a new man, not the old Randy Rust man." This really bewildered some doctors and it required us to explain to them that he really believes doctors are capable of performing these kinds of medical miracles. (For more context, we would further explain that he also thinks Target sells new necks and new heads—and frequently asks to go there in order to buy one.) Once everyone had been clued in, they would promise Randy as many brand-new body parts as he wanted, just so we could actually begin surgery.

We also learned early to warn nurses never to tell Randy when he was going home from the hospital. Nurses being nurses (as well as being normal, rational human beings) expect their patients to be thrilled to hear that they will soon be discharged. But this happy news can often lead to emotional meltdowns for Randy. You see, he loves being in the hospital. He has a TV with a remote. He has a very fancy bed that moves up and down, as many times as he wants. (Trust me, it goes up and down many, many times.) He has the attention of the nursing staff. He has a stream of family and friends stopping by to visit (the smart ones bringing snacks and stacks of magazines). Despite the fact that we warn the nurses, there are still a few who dare to tell him the so-called "good news." One unlucky nurse who did so received a swift kick, as Randy moved his leg stealthily and quickly from under his bedsheet.

To this very day, if we drive by United Hospital in Saint Paul he will ask when he can sleep there again—and complain if the answer is any different than "Another day, big guy."

While hospitalizations are rife with opportunities, even routine doctors' office visits can provide comedic material. During one such appointment, Randy watched as one patient came out of the restroom carrying a cup of yellow liquid—a urine sample. Randy immediately starting acting up because, as he loudly exclaimed, he wanted apple juice to drink as well.

Possibly the most epic of all of Randy's ER stories— and perhaps the most infamous—happened during the summer of 2000. At the time, Randy was twenty-one years old, six feet tall, two hundred pounds—and had become his very strong, extremely stubborn self. During a weekend up north at the cabin, Randy had one of his angry outbursts and punched a 30x30 picture frame on the wall, smashing the glass—and slicing open his hand in the process. We could not get the bleeding to stop, so we wrapped his hand as well as we could and Randy, Allie, and I headed to the closest emergency room, which was thirty minutes away.

Once we arrived, settled in, and waited to be called for X-rays, Randy insisted that he needed to go to the bathroom. There is no "holding it" for Rand—-it is always an immediate need. So, into the men's bathroom he went, by himself—-bloody, bandaged hand and all. After about ten minutes with no sign of him, I started getting anxious and made a few attempts to peek into the busy men's bathroom and yell to him. He proceeded to ignore me—but I sure did get the attention of a lot of random men, which is why a security guard appeared shortly afterward and asked if he could help me (the "crazy lady" he had been alerted to) with something.

After I explained who Randy was, as well as the situation, the guard went in to check on him. A few moments later, the security guard came out of the bathroom utterly (and understandably) shocked. Without making eye contact, he informed me that perhaps we should just "give him a little more time." The guard said to me, "He asked me to leave him alone; he was playing with himself." I am pretty sure Allie, who was almost sixteen years old at the time, wanted to run away right behind the guard as he left. All other avenues exhausted, eventually the only option left was for me to go into the men's restroom and get him myself while Allie stood at the door and warned anyone trying to enter.

By this time, all of our stress levels were high—and we had not even gotten to the X-ray yet (not to mention the stitches that we knew would come later). On the plus side, when the staff realized how extreme the situation had become, we were given a nice private room with a window facing the nurses' station.

With decades of experience in handling Randy's outbursts, I felt confident in my ability to keep him calm in the new private space. But, this time, he was too far gone behaviorally—and becoming more and more agitated by the minute. The window, unfortunately, provided Randy with a captive audience. Being the natural-born performer that he is, he did not want to disappoint. Consequently, when they tried to discharge him, he refused to leave and physically clung to his hospital bed demanding a hospital gown. Eventually, he upped the ante by yelling some choice swear words including calling me a "bitch" and yelling "Shut the fuck up!" repeatedly.

Reinforcements were called in, including that traumatized security guard, and—finally—Terry arrived. When Terry calmly walked in, he told Randy to get changed, and instructed him to apologize to everyone.

Randy—knowing this meant his private show was over—immediately complied, and, with a big smile on his face, chirped out "Sorry!" He then happily strolled out of the room without a care in the world.

SUPERHUMAN STRENGTH

I F RANDY'S HUMOR IS phenomenal, his physical strength borders on superhuman. We trace this incredible strength back to the early days of his childhood, when one of our techniques for calming him down was having him stand in the corner, put his arms out to his sides, and do little arm circles until he calmed down. It seemed like a good idea at the time.

One summer, shortly after he moved into a new group home, Randy excitedly told me all about the new "baby trees" that the staff had planted in the front yard. When I drove up to pick him up for his weekend home visit, I looked for the new trees but saw nothing but three piles of twigs in the yard. I asked Randy about the trees and he remorsefully replied, "I killed the trees." When I asked the staff for more information, they explained he had gotten so frustrated that the trees were not growing quickly enough that he had snapped them into little twigs, right down to the roots, with his bare hands.

Toward the end of Randy's high school career we decided to have his photo taken professionally for the yearbook, just like all the other seniors were doing. While we were waiting at the photography studio, Randy fell in love with a sample photo album covered in beautiful black leather. He obsessed about it throughout his entire session, so much so that it actually made an appearance in one of his photos (lovingly cradled in his lap). When it was time to go, Randy had no intention of leaving without his new must-have item, so the very nice photographer offered to let him keep a different—but similar—book. Not realizing that there was absolutely no substitute that would be acceptable to Randy—especially not a *brown* book when the other had been black—the photographer excitedly went to hand Randy the replacement book only to have Randy wind up and punch him directly in the stomach. The poor photographer stayed doubled over so long that we just quickly gathered our things, apologized profusely, and showed ourselves out while he continued to try and catch his breath.

That same strength, in combination with Randy's freakishly high tolerance for pain, came into play when he was once so determined to yank a nail out of a wooden board that he used his teeth. The wood had been holding his TV up on the wall, you see, and that was really hindering his plan of launching the TV down a flight of stairs. Miraculously, the TV survived being thrown down the stairs, unlike Randy's tooth—which broke as he pulled out the nail.

His insane pain threshold has fascinated medical professionals for years, constantly shattering their expected limits of what a patient can and cannot do when it comes to pain. He has performed his own "toenail removal" procedures (it is as graphic as you would imagine) so often that we have resorted to getting him monthly pedicures. Being allowed to pick out a nice, bright nail polish color has been the only reward that actually motivates him to leave his toenails on. Like women all over the world, Randy has grown to really look forward to the pampering, telling me, "I just love my *pedicares*. You know, Mom, where my feet take a bath."

He has also removed his own catheter without batting an eye. And even, once, removed his own nasogastric tube—the kind that reaches all the way from your nose down into your stomach.

Suffering from scoliosis, Randy eventually needed the very intense—and painful—surgery where large metal rods are fused to the spine. The doctors warned us how much pain Randy would be in, how long the recovery process would take, and how long he would be immobile for part of his recovery. As usual, they severely underestimated Randy. A short while after coming out of his lengthy surgery, Randy simply got out of bed and asked to be taken to McDonald's.

Dentistry has also always been a battle with Randy, so when it became obvious that he would need braces, we knew sedation was going to be our only option. Under the anesthesia he went and, a few hours later, emerged with a full mouth of braces. We were about twenty minutes into the drive home when I checked on him in the rearview mirror and was horrified to see him ripping out his entire new set of braces—with his bare hands. He was not a fan.

We did eventually get his braces replaced, but the process was not without a few more bumps in the road. Once, after finishing a caramel apple (not the smartest snack choice, I now realize), Randy somehow managed to get the stick lodged between the brackets on his front two teeth and the main wire connecting them all. Determined to get it out, he called on his crazy Hulk strength and pulled the wire so far that it created about a four-inch loop that protruded out from his closed mouth.

Randy's Herculean strength has obviously resulted in more than a few self-inflicted injuries over the years. Just last year, he mysteriously fractured his left hand (which is his dominant hand). While no one really knows when or how it happened, the assumption is that he probably hit a wall out of anger. Randy, however, has unflinchingly stuck with his story that "a cloud fell on it." Only in Randy's world could a cloud randomly fall on someone's hand—and break it.

CHURCH, FUNERALS, AND WEDDINGS

R ANDY'S EXPERIENCES WITH THE Catholic Church throughout the years have proved to be a mixed bag, but, as a lifelong Catholic, I am proud that he has finally been able to regularly attend Assumption Church in Saint Paul with us. Because sitting still and talking quietly—and not yelling obscenities—was a challenge for Randy, church was not in our weekly schedule for many years. The times that we risked it and took him, we would spend the entire Mass on edge, waiting for Randy to showcase his talent of knowing the exact wrong moment to yell out just the "right" thing.

Things soured early at the smaller parish we were a part of when the kids were young. We were told that Randy would not be allowed to make his First Communion with the other seven-year-olds because he did not fully understand the Eucharist (as if that is a concept that all other seven-years-olds fully grasp). I was so disappointed that I wrote a heartfelt and impassioned letter to the archbishop questioning whether the church fully understood mental disabilities. I pointed out that this act of exclusion also contradicted my personal beliefs—and my understanding of the faith I thought I understood. The archbishop's office responded with a retraction and agreed that, yes, of course Randy could make his First Communion.

The joke was on them, though, because when I caught wind of the *real* reason the parish had denied him in the first place, I just started taking Randy up to receive Communion on my own. (Apparently there had been some families who did not want Randy to make his First Communion with their children because they were concerned he could cause a disturbance.) He never did officially make his First Communion, but I have hope that God will give us a "pass."

While Randy is able to attend church with us regularly, it would be a stretch to say that he *enjoys* it. In fact, his usual mantra as we walk through Assumption's big front doors is "Just get church done and over with." And while, overall, recent years have been much better in terms of his behavior, Randy still likes to keep things interesting.

One Sunday, there was a different female singer than usual so Randy let his opinion be known as he yelled out, "She is too loud; it's hurting my ears." And there was the time when he shouted out the simple, but effective, "I just don't like church!" Or the crowd favorite, "I am earning the lady magazine with good behavior at church."

But Communion time, or "getting the chip" as he calls it, has always been the high point of Mass for him. After all, when it's snack time—and a sign that the end is near— what's not to like? He likes to mix up the routine, though, so on occasion he has just gone for it and reached into the chalice to help himself to a "chip," and on more than one occasion has gotten distracted mid-snack by brochures and pamphlets on the bookcase at the back of the church and set his snack down while he browsed. All things considered, we feel fortunate to have been welcomed at Assumption, a parish that has been accepting and genuinely embraces all parishioners, regardless of their challenges.

We did, once, venture over to the large Cathedral of Saint Paul for a special occasion. They were in the middle of substantial renovations and refurbishment of the large copper domes that top the impressive church, so they had large TVs set up in the lobby to show more about the interesting restoration process as well as describe the history of the building. Predictably, Randy fell in love with one of the TVs. When whining about taking the TV home quickly escalated to extremely loud yelling—and physically trying to take it—a very small, very elderly usher tried to come to our assistance. We were so afraid for the usher's safety that we convinced him to give us a little space while we handled the situation.

We could tell that Randy was way past reasoning with, and we knew we would have to get creative in talking him down. So, on the fly, we managed to convince Randy that the usher had gone to get a wagon to help us transport the large TV—and somehow managed to get Randy into the car to make a fast getaway. We are pretty sure that incident was a "near miss" with the Saint Paul Police. (As you will discover later in this chapter, we were not as successful in avoiding a run-in with the Eagan Police Department.)

In terms of other church gatherings, we have limited Randy's funeral experience to mainly grandparents and very close family or friends (in other words, those who loved him enough that they would not have been offended by Randy upstaging them at their own memorial services). His first funeral was for his great-grandmother Agnes, who passed away when Randy was ten years old. We walked in and, after one look at her open casket at the back of the church, Randy started loudly reciting the nursery rhyme "Peter, Peter, Pumpkin Eater"—ending with a very dramatic "Put her in a pumpkin shell and there she'll keep, very well!" It was not exactly a reading that the family had chosen to be included in her services, but we had to admit that it was oddly on point.

As I am sure most parents can agree, it is always a struggle to find a balance between providing a child with closure and overwhelming that same child with the grief and complexities of death. The finality of it is difficult enough for an adult to grasp, much less for a child—and far much less for a child with such severe developmental disabilities. At my father's wake, we caught Randy leaning over the casket shouting, "Wake up, Granddad! I am talking to you!"

Although it may have disturbed some of the others in attendance, we learned how crucial that "visual closure" was for Randy when his other grandfather passed away—and was cremated before the services. Because Randy was not able to get his final closure, he spent the majority of the day wandering the church, opening doors to offices, and searching for his grandfather. Randy was simply not able to understand that he was gone.

Randy actually talks about going to visit the dead, as though we could just hop in the car and drive to wherever it is they are. Or, occasionally, he reasons that maybe death is just a temporary situation and he will be able to see the deceased when "they're all done being dead."

Despite the emotional toll that these losses have taken on Randy, he has typically enjoyed the actual funerals simply because he has been able to spend time with family and friends that he otherwise has not gotten to see often. Not being invited to many weddings (we truly cannot blame anyone for leaving him out), funerals have served as the majority of Randy's family gatherings. Of course, because funerals are the only family events he knows, when he attended his sister Stephanie's wedding (one of his first), he repeatedly told people, "This is the funnest funeral I have ever been to!"

That "fun funeral" took place on December 30, 2006, at Assumption Church. Randy was an honorary groomsman whose main duty consisted of escorting me down the aisle at the beginning of the ceremony. (Ushering anyone else down the aisle was a bit out of the realm of possibility.)

As we began the long walk down the aisle, Randy recognized many neighbors and friends and began to wave and yell out to them. Hoping to quiet him down, in true "mom" fashion, I "shushed" him. And—in typical Randy fashion—he "shushed" me right back, the photographer capturing him with his finger to his lips and everything.

During the wedding, we were extremely grateful to have some of our favorite group home staff members, Bryan and Jackie, stationed like "bouncers" at the door. As soon as Randy began to talk loudly about wanting to "be all done with the funeral," I raised my eyebrows and pointed to them, and that proved to be enough of a threat to keep him quiet until Stephanie and Erik said "I do."

In the weeks leading up to the wedding, we had tried to help Randy understand that he would be gaining a brother. While waiting in the drive-thru line at McDonald's, he imparted some wisdom on us, instead. Stephanie led him through the reasoning behind the new family member, asking: "If I marry Erik, and you are my brother, what does that make Erik?" Randy thought about it for a moment and responded, "Happy?"

Happy was correct—even though it may not have been the answer we expected. We were happy on another account because the TS genetic marker had been found. Randy's gene was identified on TSC2 and now the girls could be tested. Neither carried the gene! Both Stephanie's and Allie's weddings were incredibly joyful events for Randy and our whole family. Being very musically inclined, Randy has always liked dancing—and did not disappoint on the dance floor at the girls' weddings. Wearing a nice (but less than perfectly tailored) rental tuxedo, Randy quite literally "danced his pants off" at Stephanie and Erik's wedding. Surrounded by Stephanie's high school and college girlfriends, and loving all the attention from the ladies, Randy was getting everyone going by jumping up and down, waving his arms in the air. On one particularly forceful jump, his dress pants suddenly fell around his ankles. Taking it like a champ, he yelled out a surprised "Whoops! Pull your pants up!" Then he took his own advice, pulled them up, and kept right on dancing.

At Allie and Jesse's wedding a few years later, he inadvertently found himself in the center of the dance floor. Most of the guests had formed a large dance circle, while different people dared to jump in the middle and show off their skills. Completely oblivious to what was going on, Randy wandered into the middle of the circle, looking for me. He looked startled—and a little overwhelmed—when the crowd started to cheer for him to dance, so Allie and Stephanie rushed to his side, thinking that they would rescue him. At that moment, the wildly popular song "Gangnam Style" came on and Randy immediately broke into dancing jumps, arms waving, with a huge smile on his face. His sisters, the would-be rescuers, changed gears and joined in his dance, providing one of the most memorable moments of the wedding reception.

But, as much as he enjoys them, Randy does not fully understand the significance of weddings. He is thrilled to have the additions of his brothers-in-law and loves his nieces and nephews, but he will never understand why Stephanie and Allison had to "grow up and go live at Erik's and Jesse's houses." Like one of Peter Pan's lost boys, Randy will never grow up. And he will never fully understand why others do.

Randy has always wanted to wear a wedding dress, and because of this fascination, one outing in the '90s became the opposite of a fairytale. Having popped dinner in the oven, I took Randy, Allie, and Allie's friend Caitlin on a quick errand to the bookstore. All was going to plan, when Randy spotted a large, rather expensive, *Martha Stewart Weddings* book. The girls were in middle school at the time, so we were definitely not in the market for wedding inspiration. As Randy's behavior began to escalate and his voice started to rise, a lovely elderly woman stopped by and offered to buy it for him. I declined her offer, but was very touched by her compassion for Randy.

Realizing Randy was not going to leave the store without the book, I quickly devised a plan. I approached a young, male employee and asked him to escort us to the car *with the book*. Then, once everyone was in the car, he could run back into the store with the book in hand. The young man appeared very unsure—and a bit frightened—by what I was asking him to do, but agreed to the role. So, as he ran back to the store with it and we took off in the car, Randy processed what had just transpired and realized he no longer had the book. I thought everything had gone off without a hitch. Until . . .

Sitting in the front passenger seat, Randy lost it. He completely and utterly lost it. My plan had not been so genius after all. He started punching the windows, screaming, and trying to get out of the car. From the back seat, Allie and Caitlin were trying to keep him in the car by holding onto the hood of his winter jacket as I tried to talk him through the situation. As I was accelerating down the entrance ramp to the freeway, Randy swung the door of the minivan open, the zipper on the hood gave way, and he went flying out of the car. I slammed on the brakes, as did several cars behind me.

Randy was in a full-on rage and kept pounding on the van while screaming at the top of his lungs. (Remarkably, he was not hurt, despite his dramatic exit from the minivan.) The Eagan Police showed up quickly, and the first police officer to arrive on the scene looked very young and naive. I got the impression that he was a rookie. I am not sure who he was more afraid of: me and my anger, or Randy's out-of-control behavior. The next police officer to arrive was much more seasoned and successful in calming all of us. He offered to take Randy back to the store so that I could get home to tend to my lasagna (which was burning in the oven by that point), and get Caitlin home to her family (with quite a story to tell them). The officer told me to go home, calm down, and return to the bookstore in an hour.

When I recovered and returned to the store, I found the two of them sitting side by side, paging through that doggone Martha Stewart book. The police officer then asked Randy to put the book back on the shelf and go home with me, which Randy did with a smile on his face. He shook the police officer's hand, said goodbye, and turned to me and said, "Mom, that was the nicest mailman." I was, and to this day remain, unbelievably moved by—and grateful for—the actions of that "mailman."

This was not our last wedding dress story, however. Another wedding dress tale is that of Stephanie's beautifully preserved bridal gown. She had sent it to a company in New York City to be cleaned and stored in a specially sealed box, never to be opened. We offered to keep it for her at our house since she and her husband, Erik, were living in Denver at the time. Fast-forward to Christmas 2007—a year after the wedding. Once all the gifts had been opened, Randy was whining about wanting more and wondering where the new bedsheets (that he gets every year) were. He wandered upstairs and found the big blue box with the veil and dress displayed through the plastic window on the front. Sure that this was one more gift, he tore it open—ripping the veil apart and throwing the dress on the floor in the process. We were drawn to find him in the middle of the crime scene because he was yelling, "WHERE ARE THE SHEETS?"

LIFE OF THE PARTY

N FEBRUARY 2004, WINTER CARNIVAL week was underway at Visitation High School. The week of fun, celebratory activities culminated with the coronation of the queen, which Allie had graciously been voted by her peers. After her speech, close family and friends were brought up on stage to be "knighted" in front of the entire school. Most of Allie's friends had met Randy and many others at the school were aware she had an older brother who was mentally handicapped, but had never seen him. Or more accurately, they had not *experienced* him. Allie insisted he be present for the ceremony, as he had helped shape and influence her just as much as anyone else in her life. While I was touched by her insistence, I was incredibly nervous for Randy's behavior.

As always, I knew that we should expect the unexpected, but managing a potential behavioral outburst on stage—in front of over five hundred people (including young schoolchildren)—was uncharted territory. After all, we know Randy loves an audience. (The last time Randy had been at the school was years earlier, when we were seen dragging him out of Stephanie's Christmas pageant because he began to scream as she sang a solo.)

The knighting began and, one by one, everyone kneeled on a pillow as the "Prime Minister" introduced us and read a short tribute Allie had written about each of us. Stephanie's knighting went well, then Terry's went well and, just as I went to kneel with Randy, he kicked the pillow out from under me and into the audience. After a moment of awkward—and nervous—silence, we began laughing, and then the entire school joined in. It was as if Randy knew people expected him to do something zany, and he did not want to disappoint.

Luckily, that was all he did and, if anything, it lightened the mood as I laughed and everyone else chuckled right along with me. Once the laughing died down, Randy and I were knighted kneeling directly on the floor. As we got up to exit the stage, Randy began to run. I tried to grab him to slow him down and, in doing so, missed a step on the stairs and fell flat on my face. We still have video of that ceremony, and you can hear the gasps in the audience—along with my brother narrating the video, saying, ". . . And down goes Cindy!" Perhaps Randy's sense of humor is more genetic than we would like to admit.

We have also had some really memorable birthday celebrations with Randy. When he was first diagnosed, little was known about tuberous sclerosis and doctors warned us that he was not expected to make it to age twenty, let alone into his thirties. So, when Randy reached his thirtieth birthday, we decided to really commemorate the milestone. We invited around seventy people: relatives, family friends, various group home staff members, and teachers who had known Randy through his schools or work programs. We held it at a popular burger joint, where Randy was working one or two days a week. (If you ask Randy what his job is there, his standard answer is: "I work my butt off mopping the floor.") As much as he detests hard work, he does love the hustle and bustle of the busy restaurant and truly enjoys being in the social environment. And he was thrilled to be there for a celebration (when no one asked him to roll silverware in napkins).

The party was a hit—we served up burgers and fries and watched a highly entertaining photo slideshow of Randy's life that his sisters had put together. When it was time for cake, however, Randy was nowhere to be found. We finally spotted him outside of the party area, talking with a group of young people at the regular bar. When Terry went over to get him, he started to apologize for Randy bothering them when the kids explained "Oh no, it's fine; we know Randy!" It is heartwarming to be reminded that Randy legitimately does have friends everywhere. Once he comes into your life, he is impossible to forget.

One of our more recent entertaining nights with Randy occurred at the birthday party that Allie's husband, Jesse, threw for her thirtieth birthday. The party was at

Betty Danger's, a satirical country club in Minneapolis. The "club" has a miniature golf course, the first hole of which features a gigantic gorilla statue that Randy was immediately drawn to. He made himself comfortable, sitting on the gorilla's lap, and introducing the gorilla to Allie's friends. He spent most of the night growling at the gorilla and trying to get the gorilla to growl back. Any time a group of restaurant patrons were actually trying to start their round of mini golf, we had to apologize, convince Randy to give the gorilla a break, and let them play through. As the party came to an end, Randy departed after sharing a long, heartfelt goodbye hug with his new gorilla friend.

We never know what is going to catch Randy's eye and we really cannot predict the random things that will bring him so much joy, but it is really something to witness his pure, authentic happiness. Like that of an eternal child, his joy is sincere and we feel strongly that Randy's great purpose is to spread that happiness. For instance, even though exercise (not one of Randy's first choice activities) was involved, he was really feeling the joy during the latest fundraiser walk for tuberous sclerosis, dancing and singing along with the "Teddy Bear Band" that performed post-walk. He even managed to score a hat that was supposed to be reserved exclusively for the top donors—we are still not sure how he ended up with one. While we raised a decent amount of money among our "Team Rand the Man" walkers, we suspect that the hat was earned by Randy's signature million-dollar smile and wink.

At the same walk a few years earlier, he was feeling less joyful during the mile-long route around the park. Whining about being tired, and complaining that his legs hurt, he fell farther and farther behind our group of walkers. The next thing we knew, Randy was happily whizzing right by us—on the golf cart that was on call for medical emergencies. He had convinced the walk volunteers to just drop him off where the chicken wings were being served at the end of the route. He was sure joyful then.

HAPPY HOLIDAYS

RANDY HAS ALWAYS LOVED holidays and with Halloween, his birthday, and Christmas all falling within a two-month span, he is in especially rare form during these months (even beyond his baseline—which is already a truly rare form). But with Randy, every holiday is a little bit like the plot of the movie *Groundhog Day*.

For each Halloween, Randy's costume of choice is always either a pumpkin or Santa Claus, and every Christmas and birthday wish list consists of black tennis shoes and new bedsheets. Unfortunately, although he is predictable, it does not make it any easier to shop for him. While they may sound straightforward, the black tennis shoes and new bedsheets he wants are always a specific type—one that Randy has dreamt up in his mind and is only known to him. Upon opening our futile attempts, he always replies with a disappointed "You can get the other black tennis shoes later?"

On one of the odd Halloweens that Randy was willing to wear a different costume, it worked out in his favor. He and his housemate went dressed up as a giant spoon and fork, for which they won first place in a costume contest, including gift certificates to Wendy's, one of Randy's favorite restaurants. (To be honest, Randy has never met a fast-food restaurant he did not love . . . and want to eat at every day.)

Because Randy is essentially a child trapped in an adult's body, the magic of Christmastime is still alive and well for him. While we might stray from attempting to find Randy's dreamed-of black tennis shoes or bedsheets, every member of our family and friends embarks on a yearly mission to find the perfect gift for Randy—one that will receive the highly coveted "two thumbs up" response. Most of us feel fortunate just to get one thumb up because some years—okay, most years—we all strike out. So far, his aunt Janine has been the only one to achieve it as the result of presenting him with a singing and dancing Frosty the Snowman (and, boy, were they two enthusiastic thumbs up). Words cannot accurately describe the joy on Randy's face as he gave his sign of approval while jubilantly shouting "Two thumbs up for you, lady!" His enthusiasm was matched only by the joy on Janine's face.

While he may ask for new bedsheets or black tennis shoes, there is nothing Randy actually needs and, frankly, not much that he even wants that badly. As for most kids, the excitement really lies in the anticipation, the unwrapping, and the big reveal—never the gift itself. In fact, when he was growing up and his sisters did not open their gifts as quickly as he did, he would scan the room rapidly and steal them, just so he could unwrap them.

Occasionally, someone does unknowingly give Randy's perfect gift . . . to someone else. One Christmas, when Randy was about seventeen years old, we were celebrating at my brother's house with him, his wife, and their four-year-old triplets. The kids were thrilled with their big gifts from Santa Claus: life-size Barbie dolls. Randy was over the moon with their presents as well, insisting that those dolls—in their fully undressed forms—should join our Christmas meal, sitting on either side of him at the table. (We had a photo of that dinner, and in recent years we have searched high and low for it but, being one of Randy's favorites, it must have worn out long ago.)

Like most people, Randy just loves everything about the Christmas season: the lights, the decorations, and the wrapped presents—and his spirit is contagious. When Randy was young, our wonderful neighbors put up bright, multicolored lights on the big evergreen tree in their yard. Every morning, they found the Christmas lights turned on, even though they were certain that they had turned them off the night before. A little investigative work uncovered the fact that every morning, while waiting for his school bus to arrive, Randy would run over to the side of their house and plug them in. He still talks about those lights. Some Christmases, when he insists that he wants to see that tree all lit up, we have to go so far as to drive over to the old neighborhood to show him that, unfortunately, the evergreen tree came down years ago. Randy's memories truly live forever.

Another of Randy's favorite holidays is the Fourth of July. He has always been a big fan of fireworks, although, the older he gets, the more he complains about the noise and claims that they give him a headache. (That may be one of the only age-appropriate things about him!) Despite his grumpiness about scary fireworks, he loves the boat rides, the parades, and the picnics that go along with our family celebrations of Independence Day.

Fittingly, he is always up for a big slice of ripe watermelon. One July Fourth, when he was eight years old, he began complaining about pain in his ear. Since he had always been riddled with ear infections, we took him straight to the doctor. After giving him prescribed antibiotics for several weeks without much improvement, we finally insisted that the doctor flush his ear, because we had noticed that a horrific smell had started to waft from the side of his head. To our amazement, we watched as three watermelon seeds came flowing out of his ear. To this day when Randy's ears are bothering him, he asks: "Can you get the seeds out of my ears?"

When Randy was young, we spent every Fourth of July in Clear Lake, Iowa. Visiting his Mamie and Granddad (my parents) had become our annual tradition and it always included a town carnival, a parade, and fireworks on the lake. Once Randy had begun to venture out more on his own, I bought him a metal ID bracelet with his name and address on it, which also indicated that he had seizures.

One year, we had enjoyed the celebrations and then, just as it happened every July fifth, the carnival packed up and hit the road. And, like the carnival, Terry had also gotten up early to head back to work in the Twin Cities. Randy must have heard him because, shortly after—wearing only a T-shirt, underwear, and his sneakers—Randy headed out the door of the house and back toward the carnival a few blocks away. We guessed that he caught sight of the trucks pulling away and followed them out to the entrance of the highway.

Randy was picked up on the highway by a Good Samaritan, who assumed that he had wandered away from the "Handicapped Village" down the road. But, when he tried to return Randy there, he learned that Randy was not a resident and so he took him to the police station. Thanks to the ID bracelet we had recently gotten Randy, the police at least knew that he was from out of town, but that was the extent of the information they could get out of him. So they found him some shorts and took him to the bakery next door for donuts (a few times, actually).

Meanwhile, back at my parents' house, we were all awake but completely unaware that Randy was not upstairs sleeping. Like a scene straight from a movie, Randy had piled up his blankets in the bed so it looked like he was in there, sound asleep—and we chalked up his late morning to exhaustion from the fireworks the night before. While we were blissfully unaware, the police had done some impressive detective work and reached out to our local police department, who had tracked down our exact address and talked to neighbors until they eventually found someone who knew where we were staying.

About four hours later, the police called my parents' house and informed us that Randy was there with them . . . and had been racking up quite a tab at the local bakery. This was the true beginning of Randy's affection for the police, those friendly uniformed donut providers.

I feel I should mention that, because of the length of time it took the police to find us, Child Protection Services had been contacted. When we got back to Minnesota, they showed up on our doorstep to further investigate concerns of neglect. This was pretty traumatic for me, but Terry—with his dry wit and cool demeanor—assured me that anyone who spent more than fifteen minutes with our family would understand just how this had happened.

Another memorable Fourth of July at the lake involved Randy's first (and only) introduction to alcohol. Randy was about twenty years old at the time and some good family friends had invited us to come over to watch the fireworks. A bunch of kids were throwing around beers from a cooler and one, who did not know Randy (and was obviously not paying much attention), offered him a beer. Randy, having no idea what a beer was, gladly accepted. Before we could stop him, he popped it open, took a big swig, and yelled "Ick! This root beer is sour!" Needless to say, he has not had a beer since (nor has he been offered one).

Later on that night, our friends' two very large Labrador retrievers got scared by the loud fireworks and both leapt onto Randy's lap. Maybe it was the swig of beer he had—or just plain shock—but Randy did not say a word. The dogs enjoyed the entire fireworks display from the comfort of Randy's lap.

We had another eventful holiday one Mother's Day when we were celebrating with my brother's family by having brunch at a nice country club. A twentysomething Randy began obsessing about a large TV in the bar area. His wonderfully patient aunt Janine (of "two thumbs up gift" fame) offered to take him on a walk outside to help distract him and get his mind off the TV.

The club's dining room had big, beautiful picture windows so we—along with most of the other diners at the club—had a great view of the two as they strolled. We watched them walk. We watched them talk. And then we watched Randy unzip his fly and "water" the tulips lining the front walkway while facing the restaurant.

Happy Mother's Day, everyone!

THE CABIN

OUR LAKE CABIN IN NORTHERN Minnesota has been the scene of countless memorable Randy stories. He absolutely loves the cabin and is always happy when he is able to spend summer weekends there with the family. The water is Randy's happy place and a boat ride is one of the few activities that can keep Randy calm and content for hours. Occasionally, he will emerge from his daze in the back of the boat (he sits in the same seat, every time) and yell "GO FASTER, DAD!" But what he loves most about his time at the cabin is that he has the whole family together for an entire weekend of meals, boat rides, campfires, and cabin activities.

During the summers while they were in college, our girls often invited their college friends from the East Coast to visit Minnesota and spend some time "Up North" at the cabin. After hearing many Randy stories throughout their college years, these friends were always excited—and understandably a bit nervous—to meet Randy in person. They were well aware that he was known for speaking his mind, and that his first impression upon meeting a new person would be a lasting one.

We like to think Randy exceeded every expectation they had of him. Assigning some of them special nicknames, serenading them with classic oldies, and providing them with endless entertainment during meals, it was obvious that Randy loved every minute with the girls. He would hold them captive at the campfire, making them laugh until their stomachs hurt and they had tears rolling down their faces.

During one very memorable cabin dinner with Steph's college roommates, "the BC girls," Randy was really turning up the inappropriate (yet hard to keep from laughing at) comments when Terry finally told him to go inside and not return until he could be polite. With a frustrated huff, Randy retreated to the cabin, only to return a few minutes later. Trying to confirm a changed attitude, Terry asked, "Are you ready to talk nicely, Randy?" With an undeniable twinkle in his eye, Randy turned to him and responded, "We shouldn't talk about our penises, then, Dad?" That was our reminder that Randy does know what topics are off limits, but still finds a way to work them into conversation.

Another night at the cabin, Randy was hanging out while another group of his sister's friends was getting dolled up to go out to the bar. Fragrances were flying as they were putting on their makeup, applying perfume, and spraying hair spray. Randy started providing a running commentary of the different scents he was smelling. This quickly became a fun game of Randy smelling the top of each girl's head, then excitedly announcing what she smelled like. The girls were highly entertained and lined up to have Randy sniff them. First, he told Stephanie that she smelled like roses. Next, he said Katie smelled like strawberries and Ann smelled like chocolate. But, when another Katie asked what she smelled like, Randy took a big inhale, paused for dramatic effect, and loudly yelled "You smell . . . PREGNANT!" Everyone was in shock for a moment until Katie burst out laughing. Randy might be a comedian but he is not a psychic—and she was definitely *not* expecting.

Randy has grown more cautious and "risk averse" in adulthood, but back in his younger days he would ride on an inner tube behind the boat for as long as we would let him, laughing, singing, and splashing the whole way. Then, one day, after hours on the tube, Terry slowed the boat down and—before we could pull him in—Randy rolled right off the tube, throwing himself into the water. As we circled the boat back around to pick him up, he glared right at Terry, shouting, "You tried to drown me, you big jerk!"

We have not been able to get him back on the tube since.

HIT THE ROAD

DEPENDING ON THE MOOD YOU catch him in, riding in the car with Randy can be described as exhilarating, entertaining, or incredibly frightening. It is definitely never boring. He has punched out windows, tackled other passengers, and opened doors—all while traveling at sixty miles per hour down the highway. Many times, the group home vans and the work program cars have had to pull off the road and physically restrain him on the roadside. (As mentioned, this typically leads to 911 calls from concerned passersby and, inevitably, more paperwork to be filled out for the State of Minnesota.)

But the exciting car rides do serve as solid additions to the collection of notable Randy stories. On a Thanksgiving road trip to Iowa, a four-year-old Randy sat in the front passenger seat while Terry drove and I sat in back with Stephanie. (It was the early '80s, so car seat laws were a totally different story.) An hour or two into the drive, Terry dozed off at the wheel. At about seventy miles per hour, we veered off the road and straight into the ditch. After a few moments of a very wild, bumpy ride, Terry woke up, got the car under control, and steered us back onto the highway. While the two of us struggled to even catch our breath and process what had happened, Randy joyfully pounded on the dashboard, yelling, "Goddamn, Dad, do it again! Do it again!"

Less enthused on another family trip to Iowa when he was older, Randy recognized the "welcome sign" as we crossed the border. He woefully announced, "Oh my God, we are going to Iowa." (A sentiment shared by many travelers, I'm sure.)

A great example of how literally Randy often interprets things was one particular car ride in our trusty station wagon. To avoid sitting at the longest light in town, I hit the gas in order to make it through a yellow light. I tried to brace him and yelled, "Hold onto your hat, Rand, we're going through the light!"

He immediately whipped off his seatbelt, leapt into the back seat, and started frantically looking around. When I yelled, "Randy! What are you doing?" his response was: "I'm looking for my hat, Mom!"

LEAVING ON A JET PLANE

WHEN **R**ANDY WAS IN HIS late twenties and losing ground with the tumors growing in his kidneys, he was finally admitted (as I had been pressing for, for years) into the tuberous sclerosis drug study under Dr. John Bissler at Children's Hospital in Cincinnati. The study had been seeing incredibly successful results with rhabdomycin (originally a transplant anti-rejection drug) in shrinking the tumors of patients with TSC. Because Randy had already had partial nephrectomies (tumor removals on both kidneys), this was great—and hopefully significantly life-extending—news for Randy.

The only downside was that the study required us to fly to Cincinnati several times a year for testing while on the drug. While Cincinnati may not rank high on most people's travel wish lists, Randy began to thoroughly enjoy our trips there. In fact, he liked them so much that when we were planning a family trip to Hawaii in 2009, Randy declared, "I do not want to go to Hawaii, I want to go to Cincinnati." (We took a family vote. Hawaii won.)

On one of our very first trips to Cincinnati, we were standing in the TSA line—me in front of Randy with my arms crossed in front, and Terry behind him. Randy came up behind me, took each of my hands in his, and slowly put me in a physical restraint on the floor—all while calmly saying, "This won't hurt, Mom. It's just a little restraint." You can imagine the looks we got from the people around us. But there is always an element of suspense waiting to see just what Randy might be possessed to do—or say—while waiting in the TSA line.

We certainly weren't prepared with a good response the time he was showing his Minnesota picture ID card to a TSA agent and decided to loudly announce: "That is *not* my picture." I mean, we have all had some ID photos that we are not proud to claim, but there is a time and a place to declare that—and it is probably not while you are in the security line.

A more mysterious TSA line story happened when Randy was singled out for an extensive security check—including a full-body "wanding." Terry and I asked if we could accompany him out of line—and tried to explain the situation—but were quickly denied. So we watched from afar and held our breath at the moment when it looked like Randy was about to grab the wand out of the agent's hand and turn the tables on him. While we were too far away to hear exactly what he said, it seemed that after a few comments from Randy (non-offensive and totally appropriate comments, we're sure—or at least we hope), his scan abruptly ended and we were sent on our merry way.

As if there is not enough fun with Randy in the airport, just imagine the mayhem he can stir up while in flight. During another Cincinnati visit, Randy's group home manager, Toby, was accompanying him on a flight home that connected through Atlanta. Because their plane had been delayed taking off from Cincinnati, their adjoining seats on the second flight had been given away. Toby called us from Atlanta to let us know what was going on, and explained that they could probably get on the flight home, but would not have seats together. Toby then notified the flight crew of the situation and the flight attendants asked if anyone would change seats but, sadly, no one offered. Toby got Randy situated in a middle seat, and then headed to his own seat a few rows farther back. About ten minutes later, the flight attendant found Toby and informed him that the passengers on both sides of Randy were requesting to trade seats. (Oh, to have been a fly on that plane for those ten minutes. The possibilities for what might have occurred between Randy and his seatmates could range from Randy touching their stomachs to telling them they smelled like rotten eggs—or telling them he wanted to kiss their beaks.)

On one flight, I was Randy's seatmate—and I was apparently getting on his last nerve. He was in the middle of three seats and told me to move over, saying that I was too close to him. When I asked him where I should go, he pointed out the window to the wing. He was apparently quite serious because, when I laughed in response, he stood up and yelled, "Move over, Mom, or I am going to have to beat the crap out of you." Fortunately we were not seated too close to any air marshals—and this was before everyone had video-taking smartphones handy.

Another experience that fortunately occurred before the smartphone-era was on one of our flights to Walt Disney World. Despite the flight crew's announcement that we were preparing to land and that everyone must take their seats, Randy loudly insisted on using the bathroom *right that minute*. He looked around and selected Stephanie as the lucky winner to accompany him to the bathroom located all the way in the front of the plane. As his escort, it was also her job to hold the door shut, since airplane door locks are tricky and—in Randy's world—no one has time for that. As luck would have it, the plane hit some significant turbulence on the way down, causing a panicked Randy to start yelling from the bathroom: "Stop shaking the damn plane!" When the flight attendants demanded that Randy return to his seat, Stephanie called Terry in for reinforcement, but there was not much anyone could do to get a six-foot-tall, two-hundred-pound Randy off of the airplane toilet and back to his seat.

It was an eventful landing. The whole plane watched as we touched down—with the bathroom door swinging, and Randy on the toilet (with his pants around his ankles) shrieking the whole time.

As challenging as traveling with Randy may be, leaving him behind has also proved to be emotionally difficult for everyone. While the rest of the family was traveling for a friend's wedding, the group home staff took him to the library and tried to show him where his family was in a big atlas. Randy was frustrated by being left out of the trip and, to show his disapproval, he proceeded to rip the atlas to shreds right in front of some very *un*happy librarians.

THE HAPPIEST PLACE ON EARTH

AS I AM SURE YOU CAN IMAGINE, going to amusement parks with Randy always makes for a highly amusing adventure—or possibly a highly adventurous amusement. When Randy was young, we stood out because—instead of having a screaming child not wanting to leave the parks—we had the screaming child not wanting to enter.

Randy's fears were short-lived, however, and due to his fondness for Mickey Mouse (and the sheer magic of the place), Walt Disney World became his ultimate dream destination. On our first trip, in 1985, thrilled that Randy was tall enough at his early age, Terry could not wait to introduce him to Space Mountain. Because Space Mountain is a roller coaster ride in total darkness, Terry could not see Randy during it, but he could sense that Randy was tense. Terry, however, did not understand just how truly terrified Randy had been until the ride ended.

Convinced that he had been having a near-death experience, Randy turned to Terry at the end of the ride and very solemnly stated, "We made it, Terry."

Considering his many *actual* near-death scares and the shortened life expectancy he was given soon after his diagnosis, Randy's longevity has always given us reason to celebrate. We have taken additional family trips to Walt Disney World to commemorate both his twenty-seventh and thirty-fifth birthdays.

At the time of our trip in 2005, the Disney parks had begun to allow families of children with autism or other special needs to get a pass that would let them bypass long lines for many rides. This pass was a blessing for all of us families with handicapped children—the sense of relief and decreased anxiety it provided all of us with was immeasurable. (Sadly, this service was short-lived because people started dishonestly obtaining passes—some even going so far as to "rent" a handicapped child for their vacation to avoid waiting in long lines.) Because of changes to the system, the next time we returned with Randy we had to provide much more medical documentation—and there were far more restrictions placed on the pass. But, since his emotional instability and unpredictable nature are rarely advantages, we have learned to take what we can get.

On that first trip back, when the "front of the line" pass was unlimited, we had brought along a member of his group home staff, Bryan, to help care for Randy during the trip. What we had not expected was that Bryan—a six foot, six inch tall former football player—was terrified of rides. He could have kept us all in the dark about this had Randy's favorite ride not been the Tower of Terror, a ride featuring repeated straight and fast "free falls." As with many rides at Walt Disney World, Tower of Terror snaps a picture of you on your first terrifying descent— and then displays it on your way out. Poor Bryan did not realize that he had been caught on film shrieking and hiding behind an exhilarated Randy. And, of course, with his highly obsessive-compulsive tendencies, Randy wanted to ride the Tower of Terror over and over again. Bryan put on a brave face, though, since taking on the ride was probably more pleasant than enduring the dirty looks we got from the people in line who were about forty-five minutes into their ninety-minute wait times. (Especially those that we lapped on our repeat rides.)

Having a wheelchair added a whole different element of "dramedy" to the situation as well. We truly did need the wheelchair to keep Randy moving through the park. His stamina is too low to be able to walk around that long, and as he gets tired his behavior declines as well. With toys, stuffed animals, and various trinkets to distract him every few feet, the wheelchair also enabled us to avoid dozens of outbursts (which could have been disastrous in the parks). But how do you explain to a large line of people you just wheeled past when the man in the chair miraculously jumps up and happily skips onto the ride? (We were tempted to dramatically shout, "It's a miracle!" but chose instead to just quickly follow him and avoid making eye contact with anyone.)

Feeling generous on his son's twenty-seventh birthday, Terry told Randy he could pick out anything he wanted at Walt Disney World as a present—anything at all. (We all know well enough that this was not a great idea, right?) Randy declined T-shirts and stuffed animals, costume Mickey Mouse gloves and light-up wands, until he found his desired gift: one of the large cement pillars supporting the Monorail track. After thirty minutes of pleading, and pointless attempts at reasoning, we still could not convince him to give up on his dream of taking that pillar home with him. Finally, he relented and—after a tearful goodbye, which included him physically hugging the pillar—we were finally free to move on with our day in the park.

Clearly, traveling with Randy always proved unpredictable and family trips were much more successful when we could bring a group home staff member, usually Bryan, with us. Bryan had worked with Randy for years and had grown very comfortable and confident in handling all of his various behaviors. And, thankfully, Bryan had a great sense of humor—a job requirement for working with Randy. Not only did it help Bryan survive the Tower or Terror, but it also came in especially handy when Bryan and Randy shared an adjoining hotel room to ours. One night, Randy became infatuated with the Orlando-area phone book in their room and stayed up all night, painstakingly applying tape to the top of each and every page of the phone book. When that was finished, he flipped the book upside down and began taping the bottoms of the pages until he ran out of tape. After finally falling asleep to the sound of the tape roll, Bryan was woken up by Randy—who had decided he did not like the sheets and comforter on his bed. Bryan got up, went to the bathroom, and returned to find that Randy had completely stripped all the sheets and blankets off his own bed—and jumped into Bryan's.

Bryan endured a lot while traveling with us, such as when he had to physically take Randy down in a "man hug" at an outside mall in Maui. Randy had been obsessing about something in the window of a store and it had escalated until Bryan needed to restrain him. Not understanding what was going on, a man who had been tending to the gardens at the mall came over and asked Bryan if he was a chiropractor doing some adjusting because he could use some as well.

DINING OUT

RESTAURANTS REALLY BRING together two of Randy's favorite things in life—food and an unsuspecting, captive audience.

A classic Randy story took place one Sunday morning at a local pancake house. As we were being seated, making our way through the restaurant, a waitress set down a plate of pancakes and bacon in front of a man just as we passed by. Faster than lightning, Randy reached down, swiped all the bacon off the man's plate, stuffed it in his mouth, and kept walking before anyone had time to react.

Another food-pilfering incident occurred at the home of Randy's favorite dessert, Bakers Square. We are confident that Randy has set some type of record for eating the most French Silk pies from there over his lifetime, with an estimate of somewhere around three hundred pies. Luckily, he has not tried to walk out with one without paying—yet. On the other hand, during one meal there, we were seated in back-to-back booths next to a family with small children. The little girl was peeking over the back of her booth into ours, holding her grilled cheese sandwich, when our waitress arrived and asked Randy what he would like to order. Without hesitation, Randy reached out, grabbed the little girl's sandwich, took a bite and said, "Yup, I'll have the grilled cheese."

During one of our many trips to Cincinnati, we opted to eat at a nicer restaurant on the river instead of our usual fast-food haunts. Deviating from Randy's familiar spots can be a big risk—Randy often orders a hamburger and then inevitably complains (loudly) that it "tastes icky" and that he wants "to go to McDonald's where they have better hamburgers." It came as no surprise to us, then, that the hamburger at this particular restaurant was "sour," but Randy was distracted by the waitress when she asked what we wanted for dessert. Randy immediately ordered apple crisp (a close runner-up to his beloved French Silk pie). The apologetic waitress explained that, unfortunately, they did not have any apple crisp. Then she asked again and, once again, Randy said "apple crisp." She tried a few different times to find a suitable alternative until, finally, she gave up. We finished our meal and were on our way out as Randy locked eyes with our waitress and, in his most serious tone said, "Next time you will have apple crisp."

That was not the only time his love of apple crisp caused a scene. We were at a character dinner with Winnie-the-Pooh during one of our trips to Walt Disney World when Randy caught sight of a server carrying out the largest pan of apple crisp he had ever seen. On the verge of hysterics, Randy rushed through the buffet line and was so overcome with joy that he stuck his whole head down to smell it, his nose grazing the top of the dessert. The poor, disheartened staff member quickly picked the pan right back up—and back into the kitchen it went.

CAMP FRIENDSHIP
(TAKE A SEAT)

NO MATTER WHAT THE SITUATION—or how crowded the location—finding somewhere to sit down has never been a problem for Randy.

On more than one occasion when he was really young, we found Randy sitting on strangers' laps. Once, while our family was enjoying a day at a local amusement park, Randy got tired of walking around and decided to take a break, sitting down on the lap of a random man who just happened to be sitting on a nearby bench. In the minute that it took us to catch up to him, Randy had made himself so comfortable that he was helping himself to sips of the man's fruit drink.

Like personal boundaries, chivalry has also never been one of Randy's strong suits. On crowded buses, Randy has been heard asking the frailest of elderly ladies to get up so he can sit down.

Little old ladies are not his only victims. While Randy was at summer camp one year, we received a report that he had sat in another camper's wheelchair when he got tired dancing at the camp square dance. My first thought was "Oh, that's not *so* bad—he's done much worse." But then the camp counselor explained further that Randy had actually *tipped the camper out of his wheelchair* in order to free up the seat for himself.

For many years that camp, Camp Friendship, was our summer salvation. They were always willing to add staff and take the extra precautions necessary for the sessions Randy attended. But finally, when he was fifteen, Randy went too far for even the saint-like staff at Camp Friendship. The girls and I picked him up on the last day of his session and were greeted by Randy giving us two thumbs up, his signature symbol for good behavior. It was heartwarming to see him so happy and so proud of what we assumed had been a great week at camp.

We packed his camp gear in the car as the staff handed over his camp report card for the week and solemnly sent us on our way—a mood that probably should have given us a hint of what was to come. As Stephanie began to read Randy's report aloud, it became clear why he (and the staff) were in such a hurry to get us on the road.

About halfway through the report—I think it was specifically the part where it said that Randy was chasing camp counselors and hurling large potted geraniums at them—Steph stopped reading and Randy realized that the jig was up. That would be his final session at Camp Friendship.

SHOPPING, CLOTHES, AND TREASURED POSSESSIONS

MAGAZINES, CATALOGS, BROCHURES, and neighbors' mail are all among Randy's most-treasured items—at least for a few minutes until he notices they are ever-so-slightly wrinkled or bent. Then, he becomes obsessed with putting tape all over them to try to fix the issue.

Randy sees imaginary items on the pages of these materials—usually in the background—which he then fixates on. He aspires to be like the "tingly boys" (we still have no idea who or what they are) and J.R. from the iconic '80s TV show *Dallas*. Always a ladies' man, he loves Vanna White, Lesley Stahl, Mary Hart, and Oprah. He carried a copy of the *National Enquirer* around for days when Jennifer Lopez was on the cover, saying he was going to take J.Lo to dinner.

As you know, Randy also loves remote controls. Why? He will tell you it is because "They tell me what to do." Prior to any political affiliation—back when *The Apprentice* premiered—Randy obsessed over Donald Trump so much that he tried to buy the life-size cutout of "The Donald" from his local Walgreens. (They were nice enough to give it to him when the promotion was over, so cardboard Donald has lived in Randy's room for the past five years.)

With its massive size and extensive list of items, the J.C. Penney catalog was a longtime favorite of Randy's. So many of my well-intentioned friends would save them for Randy, but—when we realized how obsessed he was becoming with the lingerie section—we eventually had to ask them to stop. Every once in a while, he surprises us with that kind of stereotypical "normal" behavior.

This ongoing typical male trait of preoccupation with beautiful women has made stopping for gas station bathroom breaks on car rides a struggle due to the rows of plastic-covered *Penthouse* and *Playboy* magazines. His fascination with those periodicals, we have realized, is partly because of the beautiful women, but also mainly due to the extra security against bent and wrinkled pages, which is provided by the plastic wrap.

Once, after a long ride filled with surprisingly good behavior, Terry promised Randy a magazine at the next gas station stop as a reward. Unfortunately for Terry, Randy immediately set his sights on a "lady magazine." They argued for a bit until Terry desperately said, "We have that one at home; pick out a different one!" They turned around to find the two young female clerks staring in disgust, mouths gaping open. Terry just muttered, "Welcome to autism . . ." and ushered Randy out the door.

Providing additional material for our application to the TV show *Hoarders*, Randy absolutely loves to shop . . . until he gets to the part where he is not allowed to purchase whatever strange item he has decided he needs: a plastic pink flamingo, just one tire, a washing machine, or a black refrigerator—these have all been things he thought would go great in his bedroom. He has been on a decades-long search for somewhere to buy his own water tower or, at the very least, a personal MRI machine. And, of course, he believes that Target sells everything from live animals to "new necks and heads." (I have lost count of the number of times he has asked me to take him to Target to buy him a new head.)

Shopping trips have frequently been used as positive rewards for good behavior. When Randy was younger, Terry often took him on long rides on his three-wheel bike, to burn off some of his extra energy. Averse to hard work, Randy usually had to be coaxed into these rides and—totally unaware of dangerous situations—he had to be flat-out bribed to stay on the bike paths and not venture out into oncoming traffic.

After one two-hour-long successful ride, Randy had definitely earned a treat at the nearby convenience store. After Randy picked out the biggest Kit Kat bar he could find, as well as a soda, Terry paid for the items. Randy grabbed them and, before turning to go, got a big smile on his face. Before Terry knew what was going on, Randy leaned over the counter toward the cute, young female cashier and gleefully told her, "Bite my head, babe."

Like any expert shopper, Randy can identify stores by one glance at their signs and easily recognizes all fast-food restaurants by their logos—a technique that is especially useful since he can't read. Some of his shopping techniques are a bit more unique, though. For example, Randy usually has to *smell* potential purchases before deciding. Everything has its own scent—especially clothing—and after a good whiff he will often nod and declare, "Smells like my size."

His love of shirts started young and his collection grew quickly. At one family gathering, Randy disappeared upstairs for a while and, apparently unable to pick a favorite, reemerged wearing nineteen sweatshirts simultaneously—one on top of the other. His arms were both stuck pointing outward at sharp ninety-degree angles, and it took a small team of us to peel them all off of him. Yet, in some mysterious way, he had been able to put all nineteen on all by himself. (In some ways, that was a cautionary tale for us about just how determined he can be when he sets his mind to something.)

Black is Randy's signature color and he has an extensive collection of black shirts, some plain and others with designs or sayings on them. Being a non-reader, he's oblivious to what they actually say, but has managed to pick out some real doozies. A favorite is his shirt that features golf balls along with the sentence "Kiss my balls for good luck." Following in that same sassy theme, he owns another one with a fish on it and that says "Kiss my Bass." And then there is the simple, but effective, one that reads, "I hear voices and they don't like you." When he insisted on buying that one, we momentarily wondered if maybe he was secretly literate after all. Our suspicions grew further when he picked out one that says, "Normal people scare me."

DISAPPEARING ITEMS

DESPITE HIS OBSESSION WITH T-shirts, Randy has always enjoyed being naked. Once, during his elementary school days, Randy arrived home on his school bus completely naked. When I incredulously asked the bus driver where his clothes were, he informed me that Randy had thrown them out the window, piece by piece, while they had been en route.

Over the years, many other memorable (and expensive) items met a similar fate. A pair of specially made sunglasses were casually dropped directly into the lake during a boat ride. A metal retainer for his teeth disappeared as well. The most impressive part of the retainer's disposal? It had been cemented into his mouth.

Another full set of clothing was permanently lost a few years later, during a family dinner party we were hosting. To keep him occupied, I had sent Randy out to the backyard with some bread to feed the ducks that were swimming in the neighboring pond. It seemed to be going well, and all the children of the visiting families were in the backyard playing—until Stephanie ran back into the house to report that Randy was naked.

By the time I made it out the door, Randy had thrown every article of clothing—including his shoes—into the pond. Apparently he had run out of bread for the ducks and had moved on to the next available option.

NEVER THE SAME OLD SONG AND DANCE

ISTENING TO MUSIC, SINGING songs, and going to dances have been among Randy's favorite activities throughout his whole life. (As I've previously mentioned, he could sing even before he could speak.) Music has been a constant, in good times and bad.

When Randy was just a toddler, he was stung by a bee, but—instead of crying out in pain—he simply came over to me with the stinger still imbedded in his hand, singing "I'm bringing home a baby bumblebee."

He has always had great comedic timing—though it was appreciated more in some moments than others. While Stephanie can appreciate the humor now, as a young girl, she was not exactly laughing the day Randy dumped a cup of water on her head while belting out "I'm going to wash that gray right outta your hair!"

One year, Randy's psychiatrist generously hosted a Christmas party for all of his mentally challenged clients. He went all out, serving a wonderful dinner and even hiring a DJ for the dance. Randy tore up the dance floor for hours and when "Love Shack" came on, he grabbed the microphone and performed an enthusiastic karaoke rendition, complete with dance moves, for the crowd.

Not surprisingly, Randy has also always been a big fan of musicals. He loves The Wizard of Oz and knows most of the lines by heart. He does a mean Wicked Witch impression on command, cackling, "I'll get you my pretty . . . and your little dog, too!" I believe that he has memorized everything from Mary Poppins to Sesame Street to Grease.

Whenever Randy cannot decipher the correct words to current songs on the radio he simply makes up his own. In his defense, many of these lyrics are ones that the general public gets wrong as well. But, every once in a while he seems to just intentionally decide on lyrical "upgrades."

For example, Randy enjoys the Salt-N-Pepa classic "Whatta Man" but has always insisted on singing, "What a man, what a man, what a man, what a fucking good man." After all, why use "mighty" when you can throw in an f-bomb?

He has always sung the Journey ballad "Faithfully" as "I'm forever yours . . . bake-a-lees." We have never gotten any clarification on just what, or who, or where, a "bake-a-lees" is.

He is a huge fan of oldies, especially "Wake up Sleepy Jean, oh what pennies mean . . . ?" And the always dramatically sung "STOP in your neighborhood!" which we like to think of as Mr. Rogers's lesser-known version of the Supreme's "Stop! In the Name of Love."

LIVING IN THE PAST

"CAN I ASK YOU A SECRET?"** is Randy's way of clueing you in that he has something highly classified to share with you. It is typically something he wants to buy, a random item he found in his coupon ads, or something he saw in a magazine or book. He sticks to his usuals: a water tower, an MRI machine, or a washing machine that he wants for his bedroom. The bigger, the better.

While material things jump out at Randy, at heart, he truly is a people person. He is always missing someone—often a random person from his distant past. Once Randy has met you and made a connection, he will never forget you. You might become "old and broken" (don't take it personally; it happens to the best of us), but you will never be forgotten. Our theory is that because his mind is not cluttered with daily worries or stresses, he has more energy to reminisce and obsess about people from his past.

Without the typical high school friends, college roommates, and romantic relationships that most people accumulate, Randy's past group home staffs, grade school teachers and aides, and attentive doctors and nurses have filled his life. People who have long faded from my memory will be randomly brought up, with Randy insisting that I give them a call.

One awkward reunion happened when we ran into one of Randy's past grade school teachers after many years. Obviously a memorable student, the teacher immediately recognized Randy, and we were having a lovely time reminiscing when she asked Randy if he remembered her too. His response brought a quick end to the conversation, as he replied, "Yup, I remember that you like clean underwear."

In addition to awkward exchanges, Randy's fondness for people from his past has also resulted in an obsession with laminating pictures. After all, when you hold on to pictures and photos for as many hours during the day as he does, they begin to bend, tear, and "get old and wrinkled."

Just a short time ago, we received a photo wedding announcement from a good family friend—one of Randy's most treasured (due to her warm, bubbly personality . . . and her killer brownie recipe). Randy carried that picture around the entire weekend, even sleeping with it next to him. But, when our toddler grandchildren came over for family dinner with Randy, one of them inadvertently crumpled it while looking at it. Randy noticed immediately, yelling, "Oh no! What the heck! UGH. Ann is all wrinkled now!"

A close family member who has always been a focus of affection—almost reaching celebrity-like status in his eyes—is my sister, Debby. An esteemed pediatric ophthalmologist at Stanford University, Randy does not get to see his aunt Debby often but he keeps a large framed copy of her high school graduation picture proudly displayed in his room. And being the very first of her nieces and nephews, Randy has always occupied a special place in Debby's heart. After Randy's diagnosis, Debby even spent time serving as a special medical advisor to the Tuberous Sclerosis Alliance. It is safe to say that she and Randy have a special relationship and her visits are highly anticipated events, which Randy talks about for months and months after. And Debby always leaves a lasting impression—usually in the form of a larger-than-life stuffed animal. The last gift was a six foot tall blue creature that Randy named "Mr. Bubbly Thing." And "Mr. Bubbly Thing" was such a treasured gift that Randy insisted on giving him a prime sleeping spot in the middle of his bed, while Randy awkwardly slept along the very edge. After he started complaining of a sore neck and back, I put my foot down and insisted that "Mr. Bubbly Thing" be relocated to a spot on the floor with the rest of Randy's stuffed collection.

EPILOGUE

ANDY STORIES WILL CONTINUE forever, so although we have reached the end of this book it will not be the end of the stories. These stories will live on in everyone who has ever had the opportunity to meet Randy and share a laugh or a smile with him. He truly has been a gift to each and every one of us.

My father was one of the kindest, calmest men I have ever known, and was always there to help me through my most challenging times with Randy. One sunny day in spring in the early '90s, my devoted father drove up from Iowa to visit his grandkids.

Sadly, Randy had just been admitted to the psychiatric unit once again for out of control behavior, so their visit had to take place in the locked hospital ward. With his recurring violent outbursts—and the medication adjustments that followed—Randy had become a frequent visitor to this ward. When we arrived that day, the staff directed us to a larger group therapy room to use for our visit with Randy. As soon as we got in there, Randy quickly began to rearrange all the chairs in a big circle for us. Then, once we sat down, Randy jumped right into leading us all in a group therapy session, encouraging us to "just get all the crap out."

As we drove home that lovely day, my heart was heavy and my dad could sense my sadness as we drove past the neighborhood boys—all about Randy's age—outside playing ball together.

My wise father shared the following anecdote that has stuck with me forever:

> *Everyone has a cross to bear in life. If everyone threw their own cross into a field and was told that they could go out into the field and choose any cross, they would all come back out of the field with their very own crosses.*

Not being able to see past my own heartache, I remember responding "Not me, Dad." But, oh, how right he was. Because he passed away a few short years after this conversation, I never did get the chance to tell him that I would choose my own cross—a hundred times over.

Mind you, there have been some very dark days with Randy: days of terrifying medical drama, days of heartbreaking violence and destructive behavior, and days of serious frustration with a system that at times would rather ignore the most vulnerable members of society. But, through it all, Randy has taught us—and continues to teach us—about patience, tolerance, and unconditional love. And that, sometimes, you just have to smile.

As you can probably guess, we have been on the receiving end of a lot of stares throughout the years with Randy. We believe, for the most part, that the stares are not intended to be cruel, but rather are out of utter fascination for the unknown (which we understand, believe me). So rather than letting the stares get to us, we have learned to just smile back. Because, once you let go of the embarrassment and get over the bizarreness of whatever Randy happens to be doing at the moment, it is pretty darn funny.

I hope that this book has made you smile and shown how we have used laughter to get us through the most difficult situations. Humor continues to be a lifeline for our family and we encourage other families who feel like they are sinking to grab hold of that lifeline as well.

THE TEAM

THANK YOU, TERRY, for being a wonderful and steadfast husband for forty-two years and a loving father to our children. And thank you for suggesting the winning title.

Thank you, Steph and Allie, for being the best coauthors—and the best sisters Randy could ask for.

Thank you, Erik and Jesse, for being the best brothers-in-law Randy could have ever hoped for.

Thank you, Michele, for being my first believer and organizer of the book.

Thank you, Mary Ann, for being my writing buddy.

Thank you, Margaret, for editing the first draft of the book.

Thank you, Pam, for editing the second draft of the book.

Thank you to the staff at Beaver Pond Press for guiding me through the publishing process.

Thank you, Randy, for providing all the material for the book . . . and so much meaning and laughter to my life.

And, to each of you, many thanks for reading.

For more information about
Tuberous Sclerosis, visit:

www.tsalliance.org